T&T CLARK STUDY GUIDES TO THE OLD TESTAMENT

JOB

Series Editor
Adrian Curtis, University of Manchester, UK
Published in Association with the Society for Old Testament Study

Other titles in the series include:

T&T Clark Study Guides to the New Testament:

JOB

An Introduction and Study Guide
Where Shall Wisdom Be Found?

By
Katharine J. Dell

Bloomsbury T&T Clark
An imprint of Bloomsbury Publishing Plc

B L O O M S B U R Y
LONDON · OXFORD · NEW YORK · NEW DELHI · SYDNEY

Bloomsbury T&T Clark

An imprint of Bloomsbury Publishing Plc

Imprint previously known as T&T Clark

50 Bedford Square	1385 Broadway
London	New York
WC1B 3DP	NY 10018
UK	USA

www.bloomsbury.com

BLOOMSBURY, T&T CLARK and the Diana logo are trademarks of Bloomsbury Publishing Plc

First published 2013. This edition published 2017

© Katharine J. Dell, 2017

Katharine J. Dell has asserted her right under the Copyright, Designs and Patents Act, 1988, to be identified as Author of this work

British Library Cataloguing-in-Publication Data
A catalogue record for this book is available from the British Library.

ISBN: PB: 978-0-5676-7093-9
ePDF: 978-0-5676-7095-3
ePub: 978-0-5676-7094-6

Library of Congress Cataloging-in-Publication Data
A catalog record for this book is available from the Library of Congress.

Series: T&T Clark Study Guides to the Old Testament, volume 14

Cover design: clareturner.co.uk

Typeset by Newgen Knowledge Works (P) Ltd., Chennai, India
Printed and bound in Great Britain

In loving memory of our daughter
Sophie Amelia Kinear Hamilton

19th October-27th November, 2009

So little time together,
so long loved and remembered.

"Where shall wisdom be found?
And where is the place of understanding?"

(Job 28.12)

CONTENTS

PREFACE

The book of Job has been my companion (or my nemesis) for many years, but it is only in the light of the tragedy that forms the dedication of this book that I have come to identify more fully with Job's distress (after all, he lost ten children) and his protest (why me, indeed!). This introductory guide has been written during a difficult year of coming to terms with a deep loss, and yet writing it has been surprisingly therapeutic and strangely comforting in the truly paradoxical climate that is the book of Job. I am grateful to have had unexpected time to finish this guide ahead of schedule and to have had the support of so many – family, friends and colleagues. Much of the material that makes up this guide formed part of a special subject option on Job that I taught for a number of years, and I thank all the students who contributed insights on that course. I owe particular thanks to Will Kynes, my former PhD student, who has carefully read through and commented on each chapter and to the series editor Adrian Curtis for his helpful editorial improvements.

Cambridge, September 2011

ABBREVIATIONS

AB	Analecta Biblica
BJRL	*Bulletin of the John Rylands Library*
BZAW	Beihefte zur *Zeitschrift für die alttestamentliche Wissenschaft*
CB	Coniectanea Biblica
CBQ	*Catholic Biblical Quarterly*
CBQMS	*Catholic Biblical Quarterly* Monograph Series
CTM	*Currents in Theology and Mission*
ExpT	*Expository Times*
HAR	*Hebrew Annual Review*
HB/OT	Hebrew Bible/Old Testament
HUCA	*Hebrew Union College Annual*
ICC	International Critical Commentary
Int	*Interpretation*
JAAR	*Journal of the American Academy of Religion*
JBL	*Journal of Biblical Literature*
JR	*Journal of Religion*
JSOT	*Journal for the Study of the Old Testament*
JSOTSup	*Journal for the Study of the Old Testament* Supplement Series
LHBOTS	Library of Hebrew Bible/Old Testament Studies
NCB	New Century Bible
NIB	The New Interpreter's Bible
NIBC	New International Biblical Commentary
NICOT	New International Commentary on the Old Testament
OTL	Old Testament Library
SBL	Studies in Biblical Literature
SBLDS	Society of Biblical Literature Dissertation Series
SJT	*Scottish Journal of Theology*
VT	*Vetus Testamentum*
VTSup	*Vetus Testamentum* Supplement Series
WBC	Word Biblical Commentary
ZAW	Zeitschrift für die alttestamentliche Wissenschaft

COMMENTARIES ON THE BOOK OF JOB

I have chosen a selection of full commentaries on Job in English and made a comment on its character in each case. The commentaries are arranged by year of publication.

S.R. Driver and G.B. Gray, *A Critical and Exegetical Commentary on the Book of Job* (ICC; Edinburgh: T & T Clark, 1921). Although dated in its introduction that focuses on literary-critical issues, the philological notes are superb and it is essential reading for anyone wishing to probe the real detail of the Hebrew text.

E.J. Kissane, *The Book of Job* (Dublin: Browne & Nolan, 1939). A critically revised Hebrew text, plus text-critical and wider commentary of a fairly traditional nature.

E.A. Dhorme, *A Commentary on the Book of Job* (London: Nelson, 1967). A very full introduction. Clear and thorough with a particularly useful discussion of the Hebrew text. Translated from the French (1926).

H.H. Rowley, *Job* (NCB; London: Nelson, 1970). Although a little dated now, particularly in its literary-critical approach, this is a well-balanced, concise commentary with good overviews of scholarly debates and a distinctive approach to the evaluation of the God speeches.

M.H. Pope, *Job* (Garden City, NY: Doubleday, 3rd edn, 1973). A critical commentary airing traditional critical views, with particular emphasis on ancient Near Eastern parallels.

R. Gordis, *The Book of Job* (New York: Jewish Theological Seminary of America, 1978). A fine commentary full of detailed textual and linguistic comment as well as sound wider engagement with the scholarship. Gives a sympathetic hearing to the fourth friend, Elihu.

N.C. Habel, *Job*, OTL (London: SCM Press, 1985). Takes a final-form approach to Job and emphasizes literary issues such as plot development. Also employs a refreshing ecological approach and is particularly valuable in its evaluation of God as creator in the God speeches.

J.G. Janzen, *Job* (Interpretation; Atlanta: John Knox Press, 1985). As the name of the series suggests, this commentary is very much an 'interpretation' of the book as a whole, with emphasis on literary and theological matters rather than a verse-by-verse analysis.

C.A. Newsom, *The Book of Job* (NIB, 4; Nashville, TN: Abingdon, 1996). Literary and theological aspects of the text are discussed, including a 'reflections' section which draws out contemporary significance. The interplay between Job and other Old Testament texts is discussed.

J.E. Hartley, *The Book of Job* (NICOT; Grand Rapids, MI: Eerdmans, 1998). Aimed at an audience of believing Christians with particular emphasis on linguistic issues.

D.J.A. Clines, *Job 1-20, 21-37, 38-42* (WBC; Dallas: Thomas Nelson, 1989, 2006, 2011). A magisterial three-volume commentary with extensive bibliographies and close attention to the Hebrew text, but also user-friendly comment and discussion of each passage.

S.E. Balentine, *Job* (Macon, GA: Smyth & Helwys, 2006). An engaging and imaginative approach that draws in art and literature from across history to illuminate the text.

G.H. Wilson, *Job* (NIBC; Peabody, MA: Hendrickson, 2007). A commentary that seeks to steer a line between critical discussion, referring to original language, and accessibility to believing Christians. Published posthumously.

A. Hakham, *Job* (Jerusalem: Mosad Harav Kook, 2009). Translated from Hebrew and written in the spirit of traditional Jewish interpretation, a rich resource for which this commentary provides an accessible entry.

J. Gray, *Job* (Sheffield: Sheffield Phoenix Press, 2010). A commentary published posthumously and so treating scholarly views up to 2000. A thorough piece with a particularly useful emphasis on ancient Near Eastern parallels.

1

INTRODUCTION

1. *Outline*

To outline the story of Job, for those unfamiliar with the work, seems as good a place as any to start this short guide. Job is a righteous man on whom undeserved calamity falls. It is made clear in the first two chapters of Job (the Prologue) that the character, Job, did everything by the book. He even prayed on behalf of his children in case they had done anything amiss. Four calamities strike in quick succession and he loses oxen and asses, sheep, camels and finally his sons and daughters. In all this, Job does not waver in his faith and even when he is struck down by a festering disease he still says 'Shall we receive the good at the hand of God, and shall we not receive the bad?' (2.10). It is made clear in the Prologue that Job is the victim of a wager between God and 'the Satan' on the issue of whether Job's faith is totally disinterested or not; is he only a man of faith because of the rewards – mainly material ones – that it brings? The Satan argues that if all is taken away from him he will curse God and when this doesn't happen, after the four calamities that lead to the death of his children and destruction of all he owns, the Satan argues that if struck down by illness Job will certainly waver in his faith. So a skin disease is inflicted on Job, but still Job does not give way – he is a model of piety and the Satan appears to have lost the argument.

However, then we have chap. 3 (the beginning of the Dialogue) and in this chapter Job becomes a different person. He bewails the day of his birth and the night of his conception and he wishes he had died at birth and longs for death, such is his suffering – 'For my sighing comes like my bread, and my groanings are poured out like water.' (3.24) From this point onwards a Dialogue ensues between Job, bewailing his lot and blaming God for proving inconsistent, and three friends who are there supposedly to comfort him, but in fact offer little but platitudes. Job must have sinned, they say, because all suffering is the result of sin. It is not God who is unjust, rather it is Job who fails to recognize his own shortcomings. Job, on the other hand, is adamant that he could not have acted in a more pious way and that he is undeserving of the suffering that has been heaped upon him. His Dialogue with the friends becomes more and more of a diatribe against them and a call on God to answer for his actions. In the manner of a lawsuit Job asks God to stand trial, but then he realizes that because God is both judge and witness for the prosecution he, Job, doesn't stand a chance. He longs for a Mediator to judge between him and God, to see that fair play is done because God has proved, to Job at least, not to deal fairly with loyal believers. Job cries, 'He [God] has cast me into the mire, and I have become like dust and ashes. I cry to you and you do not answer me. I stand, and you merely look at me. You have turned cruel to me; with the might of your hand you persecute me' (30.19-21). A fourth friend, Elihu, then appears – one who being young had been afraid to speak – and he adds a few more comments on the nature of suffering until finally the climax of the book is reached when God appears in a whirlwind apparently to answer Job's questions.

In fact, far from answering Job's questions directly, God poses a number of questions to Job, asking him where he was at creation, implying that there are things so much greater than Job that he has no right to question and to which he should not expect to have all the answers. Thus God's power is stressed rather than God's justice explained. If there is a message about justice here it is that God's justice is greater than that of humans and cannot thus be restricted by human understanding. So Job does not receive an answer to his questions, although he abases himself before God and apparently repents. Then we have a happy ending in which Job is restored to double his fortunes and even makes a sacrifice to God on behalf of the friends who are rebuked by God for not having spoken of God 'what is right, as my servant Job has' (42.7). So it seems that Job is vindicated by God, suggesting perhaps that it is better to protest and to question than simply to repeat common assumptions. Job's understanding has grown – through suffering he has plumbed the depths of human existence, and although he did not apparently receive any direct answers to his questions at least God made an appearance which seems to satisfy him to a certain point.

2. *Method of Approach*

There has been a sea change in Old Testament studies in the last few dec-ades that means that anyone writing on a biblical book needs to state their method and presuppositions. There has been a marked shift from an attempt to interpret Old Testament writings in historical terms in reference to issues such as date, authorship and historical context, which has arguably run dry in the face of uncertain conclusions, towards a more literary approach that takes books as they stand, and as the reader experiences them, without too much concern for their pre-history. As with most alternatives there is a *via media* and I shall attempt to pursue that in this book. I shall air ideas about date, authorship and context because I do think that they provide a helpful framework for understanding this – and arguably every – biblical book. This involves essential literary-critical conclusions about stages of development of the book of Job, without which, in my view, it cannot be fully understood or appreciated. However, noting the limitations of such approaches and the exciting new developments that have come out of a move away from them is also a key part of my remit and so I hope to convey a sense of these changes in this guide. It was Edwin Good in his book *In Turns of Tempest* that grouped together traditional historical questions under the heading 'A Dispensable Introduction' and promoted his more literary approach under the heading 'An Indispensable Introduction'. This conveyed what he called his 'testiness' (1990: 1) about traditional concerns about authorship, date and so on and his preferred agenda (i.e. Job as a work of literary art) that found such questions unimportant and even irrelevant. It is interesting, however, that he still felt it necessary to start his book with traditional issues and it does seem to me that however much we may wish to marginalize them, they keep reappearing because they do still have an important role. I too feel that it is right to start with traditional questions that aid our understanding of the author's motivation for writing this book, its possible date in relation to other books and ideas, and the impact of any socio-historical context upon it. Having said that, the book of Job is generally regarded as a work of great literature and so readily lends itself to a more literary approach, as we shall see later on.

Another major shift of interest in the last few decades that impacts upon the interpretation of a book such as Job is that from author to reader. The recognition that the context of the reader is of prime importance when it comes to reading any book seems an obvious one, but only in the light of postmodern hermeneutical concerns has it become of true significance. This recognition has opened up a whole new area of 'readings' of Job that I shall address in the last chapter of this guide. The subjectivity of any interpretation is exposed, and one's own context is exposed. Whilst I no doubt have my own personal bias and viewpoint, I believe that a good academic training enables one to air other biases and viewpoints than one's own. Thus I hope to give the reader of this guide a rounded picture of the exciting new work going on in the field of Job studies.

3. *Plan for This Guide*

In the rest of this introduction I shall address some of the traditional issues of date, authorship and historical context which importantly includes literary-critical conclusions about the layers of the book and its redactions. In that context our key text will be Job 1-2, the Prologue. The idea of a key text will continue through the six chapters to give the opportunity to look at samples of the text more closely often, although not predominantly, in relation to the particular concerns of that chapter. In chaps. 2 and 3, I will focus on the issue of genre in relation to Job, my special emphasis for this guide, and this will also be picked up again briefly in Chapter 5 in the discussion of the genre of tragedy. In Chapter 2, I will address the issue of Job as a wisdom book, a piece of nomenclature and genre classification that has been key to the book's interpretation for the last century and a half and which is, in my view, due for some re-evaluation. For this the key text will be the wisdom poem of Job 28. In Chapter 3, I will discuss issues of genre that are close to my own heart, notably that of Job as a parody, a theory which I aired in my own doctoral work (*The Book of Job as Sceptical Literature*, 1991) and that has been aired by others too in an increasing appreciation of the literary artistry at work in this book. Examples from Job's speeches in the Dialogue will illuminate the theories aired in this chapter. In Chapter 4, I turn to the wider context of the book of Job in relation to ancient Near Eastern texts that seem to form close parallels. Babylonian material, in particular, is seen to be significant in the interpretation of Job. The speeches of the friends are the key text for this chapter including the speeches of the mysterious fourth friend, Elihu. In Chapter 5, I move on to theological issues raised by the Job text, in many ways the essence of what readers tend to take away from the book, in that it is primarily conveying key theological messages in its discussions of retribution, suffering and theodicy. I will link back to issues of genre by looking at the tragic genre as illuminating for interpreting the theology of the book. The key text here will be the Yahweh speeches, argu- ably the theological climax to the entire piece. Finally in Chapter 6, I will look at modern readings of Job and at exciting new vistas of interpretation that are opening up for the book including feminist, liberationist, ecological and psychological approaches. The Job text for Chapter 6 will be the end- ing of the book, the Epilogue, which has been so key in interpretation of this book, especially for those looking to read the book in the context of its happy ending. In each chapter there will be bibliography not just of works cited, but of further reading on the topics aired.

4. Date and Context of Writing

The book of Job has a timeless quality in its airing of universal theological themes such as suffering and the God/human relationship that makes dat- ing it a difficult task. The book as a whole is generally dated after the Exile on the basis of its theological maturity. It appears to attack the fundamental premise of exilic theology that suffering must be the direct result of sin and represent punishment from God. Job himself is a paradigm of one who has tried to lead a blameless life and is nonetheless suffering greatly at the hand of God. The friends uphold the traditional view against which Job argues, with increasing bitterness, until he is brought to a confrontation with God himself. Although some have regarded Job as a type or representative of the whole nation, the nature of the book as an individual test case has tended towards a post-exilic dating. In the light of the increasing individualism that emerged after the Exile, as represented in the book of Ezekiel, the book of Job would seem to fit that profile. There are some scholars who wish to date the book rather earlier than the exile, such as D. Wolfers (1995) who argues for a seventh century BCE dating on the grounds that Isaiah the prophet is the author, but this is a minority view. Some have gone as late as the second century for the final product, but the lack of explicit Greek influence upon the book mitigates against this. The consensus of opinion dates the book between the sixth and fourth centuries BCE (see L.G. Perdue, 1991), with majority opinion favouring the fourth. It probably therefore belongs at the end of the Persian period rather than in the Hellenistic and it is possible that late Persian ideas influenced the development of 'the Satan' figure in the Prologue. In relation to the development of 'wisdom' this later date is supported by the observation that the book is a clear critique of the earlier wisdom exercise, as represented by Proverbs, and a more literary formulation in its entirety than its forerunner.

A primary question might be: Is Job a historical figure? Scholars are divided on this question and have been since the nineteenth century with the rise of critical scholarship (see K.J. Dell, 2012). For early interpreters, especially Jewish ones for whom the characters of the Hebrew Bible had pride of place, it was the majority opinion that Job was a historical figure, one of the patriarchs and hence from that early period. A minority opinion that Job is a parable is represented in the Talmudic text *Baba Bathra* 15a, although quickly dismissed as a suggestion in that document. For modern scholarship Job at best may have had a very remote historical existence – a reference in Ezek. 14.14, 20 to Job as a righteous man, alongside Noah and Daniel, possibly reinforces the arguments for his historicity, given that the other figures mentioned are likely to have been regarded as historical at the time (although whether modern scholarship would accept the historicity of Noah and whether Daniel is actually Daniel of lions' den fame are both moot points). One interesting point that is often overlooked is that the story is set outside the bounds of Israel with Job living in the land of Uz. Whilst this almost has a folktale feel to it in sounding like a pretend place (for Uz read Oz in modern film parlance), the serious point is that this land is outside Israel and therefore Job is not being presented as an Israelite patriarch or even as residing in the land of Israel. Uz could refer to the area of Edom, south of Judah, a conclusion reinforced by other Edomite names in the book (e.g. the names of the friends, see J. Day 1995). But even if it is a real place and this is a historical story, the fact remains that Job is an outsider in Israelite terms. Modern scholarship has tended to draw the conclusion that Job is more likely to be a paradigm, used to illustrate a moral dilemma. If traditions about a character called Job are part of a wider international wisdom tradition, that might explain his extra-Israelite home. Or it may be that the author of Job saw the potential of expanding a simple mention of a righteous man in Ezekiel and so used a remote historical figure in the service of a more literary and theological exploration of key ideas.

Questions regarding authorship tend to be a focus of attention in Job scholarship since there is no explicit evidence of a specific historical event that gave rise to this writing, nor of a social situation that precipitated its production. Some would say that there is evidence that the book is a reaction to the experience of Exile which clearly led to a re-evaluation of many theological issues and arguably resulted in an increased emphasis on individual suffering (see D. Wolfers, 1995). Thus the figure of the author (even if in fact we end up positing a number of authors) emerges as the primary influence upon its shape and content. The book of Job is the only so-called 'wisdom' book that is not ascribed to Solomon or to some named author. So who the author was can only be known from the content of the book itself (see R. Gordis (1965) for an imaginative reconstruction). A more interesting question is what message the author was trying to convey or how he was using literary techniques to convey them, both issues that take us away from the authorship question. The author may have been a renegade sage, working at the edge of the wisdom tradition critiquing the easy conclusions of the earlier wisdom quest (K.J. Dell, 1991); or he may have written the book as the result of a bad dream about becoming poor (D.J.A. Clines, 1994). The jury is out on who this enigmatic figure really was.

5. *Literary-critical Concerns*

The traditional scholarly view is that the book of Job is composite, containing additions or redactions, so that the shaping of the final form may have taken place over the period of a couple of centuries. Despite its high quality as literature, it is disjointed, the most obvious indicator of that being the change in style between prose and poetry found at the junctions of chaps. 2 and 3 and chap. 42 between vv. 6 and 7. This indicates that the sections known as Prologue and Epilogue (1-2; 42.7-17) may have had an earlier existence as a separate folk tale (or some have said a later existence, secondarily added to an existing Dialogue). Even recent scholarship that is moving towards ideas of unity cannot totally explain away this sharp stylistic division. It is also a theological division in that the Job of the Prologue is patient and forgiving, whilst the same character in the Dialogue protests vigorously at his plight. Other inconsistencies include no mention of the Satan figure in the Dialogue (or Epilogue in fact), nor of the heavenly wager that seems to set up Job's situation and the contrast between silent friends in the Prologue and verbose ones in the Dialogue. A sharp theological inconsistency is that the doctrine of retribution is discussed at length and overturned in the Dialogue only to be reinforced by the happy ending of the Epilogue. One could see the different styles as a deliberate juxtaposition on the part of the author who could have composed both prose and poetry, deliberately using one as a foil to the other. Maybe he wanted to state, on a theological level, that the kind of reaction Job showed in the Prologue is unrealistic and so set up the deliberate disjunction between prose and Dialogue to express this. Perhaps he wanted to make the point that so-called comforting friends can be less than comforting and can become tiresome and dogmatic. And perhaps the happy ending is a deliberately ironic postscript to follow the long discussion that takes up the bulk of the book. This idea of deliberate juxtaposition for dramatic and ironic effect is perhaps a more attractive idea to modern ears (e.g. E. van Wolde (1997) who shows the book of Job to be full of deliberate ambiguity and irony arguing for unity largely on the basis of imagery or word-play shared between the sections) than that of carving the book up too much. A unified reading is more along the lines that I will take in this guide – but an explanation is certainly necessary for this phenomenon of radically differing styles and theological concerns between the two main sections of the book.

Another pointer to Job's composite nature is that different sections of the book seem also not to fit the main structural or theological thrust of the whole work. So the speeches of Elihu appear at a strange juncture in chap. 32 after Job has just delivered his final plea and after it seems that Dialogue with friends is over. Nor is Elihu introduced in either the Prologue or Dialogue – he appears unannounced and recedes again at the end with no comment being made on his appearance or departure. This has led scholars to think that these speeches are secondary, especially as their theological content appears to be of a lesser quality than much of the Dialogue and indeed God speeches, largely because they are repetitive of both of them. Another possible later addition is chap. 28, because its style as a hymn to wisdom is odd in the context of the speeches that Job and the friends have been uttering. Also the book seems overall quite anti-wisdom, so why have this positive assertion of the place of wisdom in the world (even if it is elusive) especially in Job's own mouth? The second speech of God has also come up for consideration as a secondary addition, although I think that the arguments for this are weak and that such a premise is not necessary. There is a more general problem here that there can be an obsession with consistency, both stylistic and theological, that may not have been in the mindset of an ancient author. There is a danger of modern tidy minds imposing their orderliness upon a work that is essentially somewhat disordered. This point is very apparent when it comes to the dislocation of the third cycle of speeches in Job, which has caused many scholarly sleepless nights. Towards the end of the third cycle, the friends and Job seem to be making the wrong arguments and contradicting themselves and there is no third speech of Zophar. Was this a scribe who had also had too many late nights? Is there an error of transmission here? Or do we have to cope with this kind of disorder as a deliberate part of the author's intention? D. Wolfers (1993) has suggested that there are in fact only two speech cycles in Job, rather than three, with the material attributed to Job in the text being entirely in keeping with his point of view. P.L. Redditt (1994) argues similarly that the speeches attributed to Job do belong to him – Job is simply vacillating over the possibility that the friends are right after all.

One issue is the motivation for making additions. When one looks more widely at biblical books the process of addition seems to be a natural one in the context of biblical writing and before the closure of the canon. It may be that, because in the modern world we tend to think of authors writing a book as a unified whole from the start and because we value leaving original material as it is rather than changing it, we find such a biblical mindset hard to understand. Yet whenever a text is expounded to a fresh audience in midrashic (for a Jewish audience) or sermonic (for a Christian audience) terms, for example, it is changed and speaks afresh. It may be that changes were made to this text in the interests of making it speak to later concerns of later audiences. There may have been a concern with toning down some of the sentiments found in the book. For example, the Elihu speeches could be seen as an attempt to strengthen the force of traditional argument, as already found in the friends' speeches, and to leave Elihu with the final word after Job has spoken and before God appears. Elihu reinforces points such as that God only punishes the wicked and not the righteous so Job must have sinned, and that virtue is rightly rewarded by God and wickedness ultimately punished despite seeming temporary prosperity. Elihu also makes the point that suffering often has a disciplinary aspect – for the righteous to keep them from pride or self-righteousness, for the wicked as a warning and preparation for more that is to come. If there is a separate author of this section (or as R. Gordis (1965) likes to think, the same author adding these speeches in his old age) then presumably his motivation for adding them would have been an attempt to improve on what was already there in the arguments of the friends. The speeches have been very differently evaluated by scholars with some seeing them as repetitive and unnecessary, others almost regarding them as the pinnacle of the book. In the light of such different views it is hard to know whether they are an improvement to the book or a distraction. In any case they are there and thus we have to work out a way to deal with them. If they are part of the work of the original author the problem remains of his not introducing this character and using many of the same arguments used by the friends, albeit in the new context of a young outsider who felt impelled to speak out. Wolfers (1995) is amongst those who argue for the originality to the main author of the Elihu speeches. Again we are back to the point about consistency and what digressions may or may not have been acceptable to an ancient author.

Perhaps one of the most knotty literary-critical problems is that of the appearance of the Satan in the Prologue and his apparently key role there in setting up one of the major issues of the book – that of disinterested right-eousness – but then his disappearance from both Dialogue and Epilogue. In many ways Prologue and Epilogue are two halves of a whole (with a gap in the middle) in that they are both in prose. They both have folktale-like qual-ities such as the exact doubling of Job's possessions between Prologue and Epilogue. I have argued elsewhere (Dell, 1991) that the idea of the Satan passages as an addition from the late Persian period may well make sense and that if we actually subtract these passages from the Prologue, although the story is changed, it still makes sense. However, I find myself less per-suaded now by that argument in that it does involve considerable carving up of the text, and it does very much change the nature of the plot, which otherwise reads in a fairly united way, despite these disjunctions. Another point is that there are a number of features of the Epilogue that do not tie up with the Prologue, for example, the non-doubling of the number of Job's children and the emphasis on the beauty and inheritance of his daughters, no mention of his wife, nothing about the healing of the disease inflicted by the Satan in the prologue and a major feature of Job's complaints in the Dialogue. One can either see these omissions as indicators that the Satan passages in the Prologue are indeed later, or one can alternatively see them as poetic licence on the part of the author who was not concerned to men-tion these aspects. Again we are back to the point about consistency and it seems to me that many redactional conclusions are based upon modern standards of consistency that ancient authors may not have shared. Having said that, I still think that literary-critical observations such as this do high-light problems with plot inconsistency and possible disjunction (whether deliberate or not) of which we, as readers of Job, need to be aware. It may well be that the book is the composite product of a number of hands over a period of a few centuries and that the final form is different from the original intention of a main author. That seems to be the pattern found in other Old Testament books and may well have been the way books came together in another time and a different context. These possibilities need to remain open as serious ones. Perhaps the difference of approach nowadays is that scholars tend to be less dogmatic about a particular reconstruction being right or wrong.

6. *Final Form Reading*

Job is a complex jigsaw that many have sought to put back together in various ways. In the light of the uncertainty over the process by which the text came together and of increasing interest in the final form of biblical books, recent scholars have concerned themselves with the structure and integrity of the whole book rather than spending time on deciding earlier and later versions (e.g. Clines, 1989, who prefers not to speculate on 'insoluble problems'). This has highlighted issues of plot development (N.C. Habel 1985) and drawn attention to structural patterns such as schematization and symmetry (Y. Hoffman 1981) previously unnoticed by scholars. It has led to an increased interest in literary concerns and moved attention away from literary-critical issues which have been deemed largely inconclusive. In contrast to earlier attempts to carve up the book, Habel has found a striking coherence in the overall pattern of the book, finding the Elihu speeches for example to be an integral part of the plot functioning as a foil to the speeches of Yahweh and he describes the whole as a 'paradoxical totality' (p. 9). This is certainly the direction in which modern scholarship is moving, and although there are modern scholars concerned to continue to stress the importance of redaction (G.H. Wilson (2000) and L. Fisher (2009) for example), others have tried to move away from such concerns to other potentially more interesting ones. One example is the work of D. Iwanski (2006) who finds Job's intercessory role as a unifying feature of the book of Job and who rejects the usual mooted secondary redactions, also downplaying the disjunction between prose and poetry in the book. This kind of thematic approach is another alternative to a more literary approach such as that of Habel.

7. *Job 1-2 The Prologue*

The first thing that we learn about Job is that he lives in the land of Uz, the second his name. Then the key theme is introduced, that of Job's blamelessness, uprightness and fear of God. This gives us the starting point for the whole issue of the book which is what happens when a righteous man such as Job is exposed to great suffering. The next fact we learn about Job is his progeny (a sign of blessing in Hebrew thought), followed closely by his goods which are measured in terms of numbers of sheep, camels, oxen, she-asses and the attendants to manage them (also a sign of his righteousness as wealth was regarded as a reward for good behaviour). By the end of verse 3 we have learned that 'this man was the greatest of all the people of the east' – it seems that it is in the east that wisdom is nurtured and from which it originates. This is praise indeed for our unlikely hero. The nature of Job's godfearing comes out strongly in the next vignette which has the sons and daughters of Job holding regular feasts. Job's concern that they might have sinned comes across in his offering of sacrifice after such events on behalf of his offspring – some might say that this is over-meticulous concern as a parent on his part, although perhaps the key point that is being emphasized is his desire to please God at all times.

At this point in the prologue we have a change of scene to the heavenly court. These are the passages that could have been added later according to traditional literary-critical theory (i.e. 1.6-12 and 2.1-8), perhaps to take some of the blame for Job's calamity out of God's immediate remit. However, in the interests of a final form reading, I will take this part as a major context of Job. This is like a dramatic aside to the reader. We are being let into the secrets of heaven so that we know what Job does not, that the suffering that is about to be inflicted upon him is the result of a wager between God and the Satan about the nature of his righteousness. God holds Job up as his model servant and repeats the evaluation of him as blameless and upright that we found in verse 1. However, the Satan, raises a question about Job's motivation for this righteousness; is it not simply about what reward he reaps because of it; is he only righteous because of what he can get out of it? The Satan suggests that if all his blessings were taken away it would be a different story. God allows the Satan to put Job to the test, but with the proviso, at this stage, that Job himself will not be harmed.

A change of scene occurs again and we are back with the feasting children. It is here that there is a series of four calamities, two caused by human invading armies and two by natural disasters, which wipes out all the animals, the servants tending them and finally and most dramatically Job's children. The relating of these episodes has a repetitive feel as one finds in folk tales. These calamities cause Job, apparently, to accept his fate with the thought that he came into the world with nothing and so he will leave it in similar fashion and that God can give or take as he pleases. Verse 22 is a reminder that Job never sinned or spoke out against God, and so the chapter ends where it began with a stress on Job's blamelessness.

The scene now changes back to heaven and after a rather repetitive exchange, in which God indicates that Job has passed the test of integrity, the Satan poses a fresh question – what if Job is struck down in his own person? Make him ill and he will curse God! Again God concurs and Job's fate is sealed. He is covered with sores – probably a skin disease – from head to toe. We now find Job sitting among ashes, possibly on a dung heap outside the city, reserved for outcasts and lepers. At this point a new character appears – Job's wife. She appears without introduction and we are never given any insight into how she felt about the loss of her children, except that she is clearly bitter. She tells Job to 'Curse God and die!' But all she receives from Job is his rebuke and she is likened to 'foolish women'. Again Job states his acceptance of what God metes out, good or bad, and his righteousness is reiterated.

The chapter ends with three new characters and in a sense this is the transition point between Prologue and Dialogue. These are the friends who come from far and wide to meet and comfort Job. Here we have a positive picture of three loyal friends who, when they see Job, are distressed at their non-recognition of him, such is his belittled state. They weep alongside him in his grief and loss and they sit with him in comradely silence. The Prologue ends at this point and scholars have wondered whether there is anything missing here which may have formed a bridge with 42.7, the Epilogue. If there was an original all prose story then this is possible, but perhaps it is better not to speculate on material that we neither have nor can easily reconstruct.

Bibliography (By Year of Publication)

E.M. Good, *In Turns of Tempest: A Reading of Job with a Translation* (Stanford, CA: Stanford University Press, 1990).

K.J. Dell, *The Book of Job as Sceptical Literature* (BZAW, 197; Berlin and New York: Walter de Gruyter, 1991).

D. Wolfers, *Deep Things out of Darkness: The Book of Job, Essays and a New English Translation* (Grand Rapids, MI: Eerdmans, 1995).

L.G. Perdue, *Wisdom in Revolt* (Sheffield: Almond Press, 1991).

K.J. Dell, 'Studies in the Didactical Books of the HB/OT', in M. Sæbø (ed.), *Hebrew Bible / Old Testament: The History of its Interpretation*, Vol. III, (Göttingen: Vandenhoeck & Ruprecht, 2012), pp. 603-624.

J. Day, 'Foreign Semitic Influence on the Wisdom of Israel and its Appropriation in the Book of Proverbs', in J. Day (ed.), *Wisdom in Ancient Israel: Essays in Honour of J.A. Emerton* (Cambridge: Cambridge University Press, 1995), pp. 55-70.

R. Gordis, *The Book of God and Man* (Chicago: Chicago University Press, 1965).

D.J.A. Clines, *Job 1-20* (WBC, 17; Dallas, TX: Word Books, 1989).

E. van Wolde, *Mr and Mrs Job* (London: SCM Press, 1997).

D. Wolfers, 'The Speech Cycles in the Book of Job', *VT*, 43 (1993), pp. 385-402.

P.L. Redditt, 'Reading the Speech Cycles in the Book of Job', *HAR*, 14 (1994), pp. 205-214.

N.C. Habel, *The Book of Job* (OTL; London: SCM Press, 1985).

Y. Hoffman, 'The Relation between the Prologue and the Speech Cycles in Job: A Reconsideration', *VT,* 31 (1981), pp. 160-170.

G.H. Wilson, *Job* (NIBC; Peabody, MA: Hendrickson, 2000).

L. Fischer, *The Many Voices of Job* (Eugene, Oregon: Cascade Books, 2009).

D. Iwanski, *The Dynamics of Job's Intercession* (AB, 161; Rome: Editrice Pontificio Istituto Biblico, 2006).

Further Reading

Introductory articles on Job are often a good place to start reading, whether an overview of issues and themes in the book or a more textually based series of comments, and so I list some key ones here:

E.M. Good, 'Job' in *Harper's Bible Commentary*, ed. James L Mays (San Francisco: Harper & Row, 1988; 2nd edn., 1999), pp. 407-432.

S.E. Balentine, 'Job' in *Mercer Commentary on the Bible*, ed. W. E. Mills and R. F. Wilson (Macon, GA: Mercer University Press, 1994).

J.L. Crenshaw, 'Job' in *The Oxford Bible Commentary*, ed. J. Barton and J. Muddiman, Oxford: Oxford University Press, 2001), pp. 331-355.

K.J. Dell, 'Job' in *Eerdmans Commentary on the Bible*, ed. J.D.G. Dunn and J.W. Rogerson (Grand Rapids: W.B. Eerdmans, 2003), pp. 337-363.

There are also useful chapters on Job within introductions to the wisdom literature:

J.L. Crenshaw, *Old Testament Wisdom: An Introduction* (Louisville KY: Westminster John Knox Press, 2010 3rd edn.), pp. 97-126.

R.E. Murphy, *The Tree of Life: An Exploration of Biblical Wisdom Literature* (Grand Rapids MI: Eerdmans, 1990), pp. 33-48.

K.J. Dell, *Get Wisdom Get Insight: An Introduction to Israel's Wisdom Literature* (London: Darton, Longman & Todd, 2000), pp. 32-48.

L.G. Perdue, *Wisdom Literature: a theological history* (Louisville, KY: Westminster John Knox Press, 2007), pp. 77-135.

2

JOB AS A WISDOM BOOK

Since the early days of modern biblical criticism, beginning in the mid nine-teenth century and in particular around the turn of the twentieth century, Job has been classified by the scholarship as a wisdom book, along with Proverbs and Ecclesiastes. These are joined, outside the Old Testament canon, by Ecclesiasticus and the Wisdom of Solomon. Although Job has quite a different character from the other wisdom books, in that there are very few maxims and the bulk of the book is in Dialogue form, the major themes of the wisdom literature can be found. Such themes include moti-vation for piety and just retribution and emphasis on God as creator with corresponding lack of focus on Israelite history and concerns. The hymn to wisdom in chap. 28 adds to the strength of the wisdom classification. However, Job is not generally seen as straightforward wisdom, but rather as 'wisdom in revolt', a development away from the certainties of the book of Proverbs towards a more drastic questioning of the presuppositions of the wisdom quest. So the Job problem arises in fact when the system of just retribution appears to go awry and when the most God-fearing character imaginable falls on desperately hard times. It is seen, therefore, as showing that wisdom as an understanding of the world itself changed and developed and the book is often seen in partnership with Ecclesiastes which takes a further step into a more negative pessimism about life and the possibility of fairness than even Job does (J.F. Priest, 1968). Outside the canon in Ecclesiasticus and the Wisdom of Solomon that sense of unfairness seems to have been lost as both books represent more mainstream wisdom ideas, with Ecclesiasticus promoting proverbial wisdom as Proverbs does and equating wisdom with law and the Wisdom of Solomon elevating the role of Woman Wisdom as found in Proverbs 8. One might ask why the more questioning developments of Job and Ecclesiastes did not pervade later wisdom literature, and the answer seems to be that it was a phase that did not last.

In this chapter I wish to question some of these presuppositions. Although Job shares certain themes of wisdom such as an interest in just retribution, which after all makes up much of the bulk of the Dialogue and does presuppose God as creator rather than redeemer of Israel, I will argue that there are other key elements which indicate links with a wider thought-world. Whilst there are links with the wisdom quest, it is possible that a narrow definition as 'wisdom literature' has had the effect of making us read Job in a certain way, too tied to that classification. Furthermore whilst a questioning spirit seems to link the book with Ecclesiastes, I will argue that the latter author has a very different agenda and mode of expression and that the links between the two are not as close as has been suggested by some scholars.

1. *Solomonic Attribution*

One basic point to start with is that Job is not ascribed to Solomon, nor indeed to anyone. This immediately picks it out as different from the other wisdom books. Proverbs is ascribed to Solomon more than once (1.1; 10.1) and even the ascription to Hezekiah in 25.1 is in relation to 'copying' the proverbs of Solomon. Although many do not take these attributions literally today and see them as honorific and authoritative more than anything else, they tell us something about how the books were perceived in the ancient world. The book of Ecclesiastes also contains a rather cryptic Solomonic attribution, which is rarely taken at face value and the author is thought rather to be Qoheleth, the preacher or teacher mentioned in 1.1. However the very presence of the attribution is interesting (in 1.1 and 1.12) and the Solomonic theme is pursued furthermore in the 'royal testament' section in chaps. 1-2. Job on the other hand contains no such link and no historical royal link at all (even if some scholars argue for royal traits in Job's personage (e.g. A. Caquot, 1960)). He is even located outside Israel in the land of Uz and the description of him in the Prologue is in nomadic terms of measuring wealth in relation to number of sheep and cattle.

2. *Form-critical Classification of Job as Wisdom*

'Wisdom' is not only a set of ideas, 'wisdom literature' is a set of books and 'wisdom' is also a genre in form-critical terms. It is in these terms also that Job has been classified as wisdom in the past, a view that I have challenged in previous work (K.J. Dell, 1991) and will continue to do! Form criticism, although it may well have its shortcomings, has been a major influence upon how we classify and understand texts from small pieces to larger scripts and whole books. When we actually narrowly start to classify Job in terms of the three elements that make up a 'genre', i.e. form, content and context we start to see Job's limitations as a wisdom text. I am using Proverbs as a 'control' here, as the first and leading text of wisdom literature (cf. Dell, 2000).

On a formal level Job contains virtually no proverbs, the staple genre of Proverbs. Also lacking from Job are any instruction texts as found in particular in Proverbs 1-9 and paralleled in Egyptian literature of a similar type. There are small amounts of autobiographical (and biographical) narrative in Proverbs, and there are the narrative sections of Job, but they are never autobiographical. Rather, the autobiographical parts come when we are in the poetic Dialogue and both Job and the friends are talking about their personal experience. The figure of Wisdom so dominant in Proverbs 1-9 is also lacking from Job – the only possible link is with Job 28, but there Wisdom is not in fact speaking, rather it is perceived in fairly abstract terms as being unattainable (see key text below). So the main genres of Proverbs are clearly lacking in Job. In their place we find prose narrative, with heavenly scenes – this is certainly not a wisdom feature and would normally belong to apocalyptic/eschatological type literature. We find Dialogue as the primary form, laments of various types, legal-style pleas and other sections of long speeches from both Elihu and God. Furthermore there are exchanges between Job and God, in the form of direct addresses from one to the other, a genre that is certainly absent from Proverbs. On a formal level then Job does not seem to be displaying the main characteristics of Proverbs.

Taking the comparison on to Ecclesiastes, it is interesting to note that none of the main forms of Job are found there. There is no prose narrative of any length – only short biographical ones resembling those in Proverbs – and no Dialogue. Rather in Ecclesiastes there are large sections of proverbs. Often the author adds an interpretative comment to a proverb (e.g. 8.6 is commented on in 8.7). His distinctive style is this midrashic personal comment and catch-phrases which keep being repeated, the most famous one being 'vanity of vanities' (1.2). So in some ways Ecclesiastes is closer formally to Proverbs in that proverbs usually provide the starting point of his reflections (and in 12.9 he is said to have enjoyed arranging them) and short illustrative parable-style narratives are also a part of his remit.

On the level of content, that of Proverbs is very diverse, covering topics from the acquisition of wealth to family discipline and communication. These topics are always in the context of righteous or wicked behaviour and contrasts are drawn between the wise man and the fool. This is where just retribution is key as all aspects of life relate back to reward for good behaviour and punishment for wicked acts. There is a deeper theological aspect of this retributive order as it underlies the whole of life. God is seen as creator who set up an order in the world which is reflected in nature and in human society. Human beings then through their ethical behaviour can tap into a wider order in the world and that ultimately links up with God's will for the world and for humanity. Most things are cut and dried in

Proverbs and there is a certain 'black and white' nature to it, but there is at times a recognition that experience can be contradictory and that events are sometimes ambiguous. This is sometimes simply down to the failure of human beings to comprehend everything – at the edges of human understanding is God who mediates his knowledge through the figure of wisdom whom human beings should follow and to whom they should listen to acquire the very wisdom that they seek. Proverbs believes firmly in the reward of the good and punishment of the wicked involving material and societal rewards. This is perhaps where the closest link comes with the Job of the Prologue who is a good man and so hence has vast wealth, the reward of many offspring and a high standing in society. Proverbs has a very positive view of life and that is shared by Job at the beginning when good health, many friends, children, possessions and a healthy fear of God characterize his existence. Proverbs is confident in the strength of its own quest and sees it as the path to life itself rather than death. It is when this confidence is undermined as in Job that problems seem to occur.

There are clearly some links with the content of Job. The starting-point of the story of Job is very much in line with the ideals and outlook of the wisdom quest. The first question that is raised in Job – in the wager between God and Satan – is Job's motivation for piety. Is he simply 'in it' for what he can get out of it? It is interesting that for Proverbs that is not a question that comes up, in that it is simply presupposed that pious and wise behaviour will lead to good things and that people are right to follow that path. Whilst the doctrine of just rewards is very much aired in Job – and maintained by the friends in the Dialogue – the thrust of the book is actually in the demolition of the doctrine. The Job issue is that the system is clearly not working in Job's case. A pious man suffers both the loss of his goods and family and his own health – how can this be explained in relation to reward of good behaviour? It is this issue that dominates the Dialogue and so whilst it may spring from a wisdom outlook, it soon moves away from it. Certainly Job ceases to believe that life is the supreme good and he longs for death or at least release from his suffering. Either Job is 'wisdom in revolt' or it is actually breaking outside the bounds of wisdom in its challenge. The happy ending Epilogue seems to reinstate the proverbial worldview with the eventual reward of Job with wealth and new family. However, after the whole system has been so radically questioned, it cannot but sound like an ironic postscript at the end of the day.

In relation to Ecclesiastes, although there is a shared spirit of questioning of wisdom in both books, the questioning of Ecclesiastes lacks the spirited vigour of that of Job. Job still wants to believe in a just God and is outraged at the conflict of his experience with all that he has always believed. He longs for the past relationship with God that he had enjoyed and he wishes to argue his case directly with God – towards the end of the Dialogue that becomes his main plea and his obsession. Ecclesiastes on the other hand has come to a more resigned pessimism about God and his dealings with the world. The author's mood is one of acceptance. The poem on time in chap. 3 indicates a lack of human control over the outcomes of human life. The fact that death relativizes everything for him, including the attempt to be wise, casts a resigned shadow over all his other thoughts. Job talks about death and in contradictory style at once longs for it and then dreads it, but it does not make his quest to understand null and void. The retribution question is, of course, shared by both books, but the ways in which they explore it are very different.

On the issue of context, here we enter a heated debate when it comes to Proverbs. However, it is clear that the contexts of teaching and providing ethical terms of reference are key whether in family, clan, court, school or temple. There is a related issue about how theological the context of Proverbs is. I have argued elsewhere that Proverbs is more imbued with a religious context than many have thought (Dell, 2006), but, having said that, many proverbs do not mention God and are about practical advice to human beings. Given that Job does not have that nature of practical advice, it has a very different character. Its whole context is the theological one of retributive justice and whether or not it works. Following on from that it explores issues of suffering and relationship with God. It therefore moves a long way from its starting-point in the basic proverbial worldview. As to the contexts of teaching or providing ethical advice, whilst all stories provide exemplars from whom we can learn – and Job is no exception on this front – there is a question whether this story is told primarily to teach or provide ethical advice. R.N. Whybray writes that the basic intention of the author was not related to wisdom: "The author's purpose…was, in a stricter sense, to put forward in the form of a Dialogue in which alternative points of view are presented, his own understanding of the nature of God, together with a radical reassessment of the conventional expectations of God current in his time." (2005: 195) In fact the book of Job is ultimately about the triumph of experience over all the best attempts to teach wise behaviour. It is only because the righteous Job experiences such hardship that he questions the wisdom presuppositions of the friends – they labour to uphold the theory, whilst the praxis tells Job otherwise. If Job was written in circles of 'the wise', then the author was probably a renegade sage on the edges of the wisdom quest, for the book is certainly not mainstream like Proverbs.

If Ecclesiastes was written in circles of 'the wise', as indeed the Epilogue in 12.9-14 suggests, perhaps one would not be so surprised. Again, the sage may have been rather on the edge of mainstream, but the grounding of the book in the proverbial wisdom of the wise does seem to bring it closer to the heart of the wisdom quest. The author's goal seems to be to teach to pupils something of what he has learned of life, albeit personal and unusual. This evaluation may well depend largely on the Epilogue (which has been seen as a later addition, although it could represent the older Qoheleth looking back at his younger self (M. Fox, 1977)), although arguably the spirit of the whole book has a teaching concern.

3. *Wider Use of Genres in Job*

An interesting aspect of the book of Job is the way that it uses diverse genres that seem to relate to different parts of the Hebrew canon than simply other 'wisdom literature'. So on a formal level, there are many lament forms that parallel lament forms in the Psalms and a number of legal genres that bear a close resemblance to Deuteronomy. There are also elements that resemble apocalyptic. The wisdom literature is often seen as rather distinctive in its concerns, not interacting with other books mainly because of the lack of historical reference to events and characters of Israel's past but also because of rather different thematic concerns. And yet, here, on a literary level, we have evidence of more integration with other genres of Israelite life. This suggests, even just as far as literary forms are concerned, that Job is more eclectic than the traditional designation of wisdom literature has generally characterized it to be. This is supported by the content of Job that is also diverse. Much of the content of Job is the challenge to traditional viewpoints posed by Job's experience and suffering. In the course of his laments Job goes from cursing the day of his birth, to wishing he was dead, and to major questioning of God and God's justice towards human beings. He sees God as in the wrong and is not hesitant in voicing his protest against a deity who seems to be acting capriciously. It has also to be said that although the doctrine of retribution is a key theme in Proverbs, it is not solely a wisdom concern. At the time of the exile in particular we find it in prophecy, notably Jeremiah and Ezekiel, when trying to understand the nation's fate. Suffering must be the result of sin, they argue and that shapes their whole approach to understanding the exile theologically as God's just punishment upon the people of Israel. The context in which Job was written is essentially unknown. It must have been one in which the wisdom tradition was known and understood, but it looks likely that there was a broader knowledge of and concern with wider genres and traditions. This wider use seems to have been in part in the service of providing the kind of wholesale critique of traditional wisdom that the book offers, but I would argue that this is not its sole function and that a grounding in a wider thought-world is a keynote of the book of Job.

4. *Questions of Definition and Extent of Wisdom*

The question of wisdom literature and its bounds and wider 'wisdom influence' in the Old Testament is a vexed one. Should one keep it simple and the definition narrow (e.g. Crenshaw, 2010)? Or should one broaden it out so as to include any material that might show elements of wisdom forms or concerns or indeed context (e.g. D.F. Morgan, 1981)? Job has generally been an unquestioned part of wisdom, and on a very broad assessment that is hardly surprising. However, I would argue that on a narrower, more literary assessment, the book is not a mainstream wisdom book. This raises a question about the classification of other material as wisdom especially if the material is only being included on the basis of likeness with Job. The wisdom psalms are a good example of a group of psalms (the perameters of the selection of which no-one can agree on) that are classified as 'wisdom psalms' purely on the basis of comparison with the three main wisdom books of Proverbs, Job and Ecclesiastes. When we take Job out of the definition this might lead to a rather different selection, notably Psalm 73 might come off the list, as well as others. This raises the wider issue of whether we should be classifying psalms in this way or rather how helpful it is to do so in aiding our understanding. Many so-called wisdom psalms are actually of mixed type and an attempt to understand them non-cultically also has its limitations (see K.J. Dell, 2004). On a broader definition of wisdom we could arguably bring in many psalms that concern creation, another criterion for including Job, but then a thematic designation such as that may well spiral out of control. Wisdom influence has often been seen as one-way – from the wisdom literature out to the wider canon – but not the other way around. It is my contention that influences from outside, whilst not extensive, have come into wisdom (notably into Proverbs 1-9, see Dell, 2006) and perhaps most notably into Job.

5. *Cross-fertilization of Ideas*

A related issue is influence across the canon. It has long been held that sections of the canon fall into different genre categories such as law, prophecy, wisdom, historical books. In some ways the three-fold division of the Jewish canon assists this, but traditionally the number of different areas is greater and scholars tend to be experts in one area or another. Increasingly, however, connections across diverse genres are being recognized. Contextual conclusions tended to be very tied to these genre conclusions, so that priests would be one circle around the temple, very different from the more radical prophets on the street corner, or the sages in their courtly wisdom schools. These contextual caricatures are starting to break down in the light of links seen across material of different genres, helped in part by the debate on intertextuality and the recognition of resonances of one text with another from unlikely sources (e.g. echoes of Genesis 1-3 in Ecclesiastes). It is interesting that older scholars pursued inter-textual connections largely in the service of discussions of date and relative development of ideas. Interest in these connections has resurfaced again, but in a rather different context that is not as concerned with reconstructing actual historical connections as with seeing literary resonances and echoes a more literary approach is beginning to break down divisions made on older historico-critical grounds and is opening up fascinating connections between texts. Job is no exception as we shall see below. Having said that, on a historical level, it may mean that the author of Job had a wider thought-world at his disposal and used a wide range of texts to bounce off with his own ideas. In particular my finding is that he uses such texts to help Job to express some of his more radical ideas in the Dialogue through the medium of parody (see Chapter 3).

6. *The Wider Form-critical and Intertextual Context of Job*

a. *Psalms*

It is clear that Job has much in common with lament genres as found in the Psalms. His speeches often form extended laments and air similar content to many psalms of lament. The recalling of past good times with the Deity, the question of why such abandonment now, the bewailing of one's lot, all these are characteristic of lament genres. Whilst some scholars went further and characterized the whole of the book of Job as a 'dramatized lament' (C. Westermann, 1981), my own work (K.J. Dell, 1991) has focused on the form-critical relationship of texts, notably in the speeches of Job himself, with texts from the Psalms, noting in particular the way in which the author of Job uses such texts in order to borrow the form but overturn the content and more often than not change the context too (see Chapter 3). This suggests that the author was aware of what standard laments looked like and wished to 'reuse' or 'misuse' them in the service of a dramatic message that he wished to convey. The lament genre was an ideal one for the author to use because it conveyed both the standard sentiments that Job had in common with lamenting psalmists, but also was a helpful vehicle by which the author could express something different to lament psalms. For example, whilst lament psalms gave God the benefit of the doubt, for Job, God was his enemy. God had turned against him for no just reason that he could imagine. Even general sentiments about the human condition are turned into challenges to God. This brings us to the most well-known overturning of a psalmic text – of Psalm 8.4 in Job 7.17-18. Whereas the Psalmist looks in awe at the elevation of humans in the eyes of God and their favoured position in the world, Job, using the same form and expression, changes it to indicate that human beings are indeed in pride of place in God's desire to torment and trouble them by constant attention and visitation.

The noting of a virtual citation of an actual text, such as Psalm 8.4 in Job 7.17-18, rather than simply of the form-critical parallel leads us on to the issue of intertextuality. As W. Kynes (2012) argues, the presence of such citation from the Psalms with the purpose of changing the meaning is quite extensive in the book of Job. Some of the allusions, such as the well-noted Psalm 8.4 / Job 7.17-18 parallel, are stronger than others such as the possible allusion to Psalm 8.5 in Job 19.9. Kynes finds particular connections and echoes between verses of Job and verses of Psalms 1, 8, 39, 73, 107 and 139 in particular. According to Kynes, although it is often the character of Job who is subtly changing the meaning of the psalm passage, it can also be that the same psalm is used in the mouths of other characters, but not necessarily with the same challenge to its meaning. Sometimes the nuances and tensions of meaning found in a Psalm can resonate in the differing perspectives of characters in Job. For example, the question, "What is humanity?" at the centre of Psalm 8 is ambiguous, since humans are presented as lowly in contrast with the majestic heavens in Psa. 8.3 but as only a little lower than the angels/God in v. 5. Though Job parodies the exalted place of humanity on one side of this tension in 7.17-18, Kynes argues that he does so not to reject that truth, but to accuse God of not treating him with the dignity the psalm suggests he deserves. For Kynes, Job's positive understanding of the psalm's anthropology is confirmed by the fact that in response, both Eliphaz and Bildad return to the question from the psalm (15.14-16; 25.5-6), but instead emphasize the low place of humanity in relation to the heavens. Bildad even uses the words "moon" and "stars" just as in Psa. 8.3, but then compares humans to maggots and worms. Thus, the psalm acts as a locus for the debate between Job and his friends, which takes on a hermeneutical aspect as they each interpret its central tension in different ways to further their arguments. Though the characters interact with a wide range of psalms intended for praise, supplication, and instruction, Job appears consistently to use them as a means to make his argument against God, often through parody, while the friends appeal to them to try and silence Job's complaints. This suggests that such texts were important for the author and that he was deliberately using them as a framework for presenting his work. How that may have happened historically is perhaps more of a conundrum, with the dating of the Psalms being a hazardous business at the best of times, but it is likely that most of the echoed psalms precede Job in some form (possibly oral) and form a backdrop for the author to use.

This might suggest a wider context than simply wisdom or renegade sage circles. It is often said that the wisdom literature is non-cultic (argued against by L.G. Perdue, 1977), and it is clear that in the mainstream wisdom books of Proverbs and Ecclesiastes the cult is of little concern (with only one real exception in Proverbs 3). However, in Job it appears to be a different story – if not an interest in cultic matters, a familiarity with the psalms would seem to ground the author in a broader base of influences.

b. *Deutero-Isaiah*

It is often said that Deutero-Isaiah is the most psalmic of the prophets in that much of his style is poetic. Many of his oracles read as psalms of thanksgiving, which would often follow a lament in the psalter, in that many psalms are a mixture of the two (e.g. Psalm 22). It is interesting, in the light of this observation, that comparisons have been made with Job, whose tone is not predominantly one of thanksgiving. Such links were noticed in the nineteenth century when the discussion mainly revolved around relative dating – both texts were conceivably early post-exilic and so the direction of influence was a conundrum. This priority debate has tended to dominate concerns about intertextual links here. Robert Pfeiffer claimed that "The fundamental conceptions of Second Isaiah represent a development of the views of the Book of Job" (1927: 205). S. Terrien's (1966) detailed study reinforced this, looking at similarities in vocabulary and idiom and three key themes – divine transcendence (cf. Job 9.4/Isa 40.26; Job 9.8/Isa 44.24b amongst other examples); existence or being (cf. Job 4.19/Isa 45.9, 11) and the Servant of God (cf. Job 3.23/Isa 40.27a). He argues on the grounds of omission of certain key themes in Job, such as vicarious suffering, that Deutero-Isaiah must be borrowing from Job. However this viewpoint is very subjective – R. Gordis (1965) argued that the author of Job, in dependence upon Deutero-Isaiah, applied a nationalistic view of suffering to the individual test case.

c. *Jeremiah's Confessions*

Before leaving the prophetic genre, another interesting point of contact is that between Job's laments and Jeremiah's confessions. Here we are in the area of close textual resonances but some scholars (e.g. E. Greenstein, 2004) have broadened this out into positing a deeper relationship between the two texts, with Jeremiah serving as a key source of inspiration for Job. Some have argued that the confessions are themselves stylized laments placed into the mouth and book of Jeremiah but not part of the original words of the prophet (R.P. Carroll 1989). C Westermann (1981) argued for the generic lament genre here, as in Job, in form-critical terms. However, I see no real reason not to take the confessions of Jeremiah at face value, if not as his actual words, as expressing his sentiments. Ironically the presence of these laments means that we know more about this prophet and his inner feelings than we do of most. If we reject them as original, then what we know of this prophet starts to fall away. On a historical level, if there was contact between texts Jeremiah is likely to be the earlier text, even if these texts form part of a stage of redaction. The author of Job then might have picked up on these sentiments. On a more literary level, the intertextual interplay is interesting in and of itself. The most famous example, picked up by most scholars, is the link between Jeremiah 20 and Job 3 in which both curse the day of their birth. Greenstein points out the key differences here such as the fact that Job wishes away both the day of his birth and the night of his conception, thereby expanding on Jeremiah's theme. Furthermore, Jeremiah mentions the mother, father and messenger who attended the birth, whilst Jeremiah impersonalizes such mention, talking of 'knees', 'womb' and 'breasts' that indicate the mother (although knees could also include the father) and replacing the messenger as a personified night announcing the conception. Job's negative attitude to his birth comes out in the way he sees his adult self in the description of his birth, the self who has lost so much (3.3) and his negation of the possible joy that could have accompanied his arrival (3.7). Such is the negation of the day of his birth that not only is it 'accursed' but the night of his conception is too and, as if that is not enough, he would pre-fer both to have been wiped from the calendar. The author, even in this lim-ited example (and Greenstein offers us many more) has subtly changed the sentiments between one text and another enough to give a particular edge to Job's complaint. As Greenstein writes, "It is difficult to imagine Jeremiah's making use of Job's radical curse and transforming it into something so rela-tively bland. It is quite typical of the Joban poet, however, to take a biblical passage and attenuate it *ad absurdum*." (2004: 103)

d. *Deuteronomic Links*

The book of Deuteronomy is an eclectic Old Testament book, part of the Torah or Pentateuch. Nevertheless it is one of those books that contains a richness that enables one to see all kinds of influences upon it. It has quite commonly been suggested that there is 'wisdom influence' in its pages (most famously M. Weinfeld, 1972) and there are some points of comparison with Proverbs 1-9 (notably Deut. 6:6-8, of Prov. 3:1-4; 6:21-2; 7:1-3 which concern affixing teaching to one's body – see Dell, 2006). This might well indicate the wider interchange of ideas going in both directions that I mentioned earlier. However, where Job fits into this picture is less clear, whether we count it as mainstream wisdom or not. Legal features have long been noted in Job and suggestions made that Job himself constructs a *rib* or lawsuit against God (e.g. H. Richter (1959), B. Gemser (1960), M. B. Dick (1969)). This model and the idea that the retributive framework in Job may owe something to a Deuteronomic covenantal model has been recently revived by Susannah Ticciati (2005). Ticciati contends that Job is not applying or rejecting the Deuteronomic covenant in abstract terms, but is wrestling with the covenantal God himself in the light of his seemingly arbitrary behaviour. She finds Deuteronomic resonances in the Prologue, following D. Wolfers who writes "It is hardly going too far to describe the Book of Job as an elaborate midrash on Deut 28, on the whole idea of a covenant enforced by threats and promises from on high." (1995: 53). Examples are notably 1.14-19, the destruction of Job's family and property compared to the curse of Deut 28.31-2, and the description of the Satan's final affliction of disease upon Job echoes Deut 28.35 verbatim. If the Deuteronomic covenant lies behind the prologue then Job is being done out of the blessing that he should receive for his upright behaviour (compare Job 1.10 and Deut 28.12). It is certainly striking how intertextual parallels exist between Deuteronomy 28 and Job, but it leads one to ask why only with this chapter of Deuteronomy? Has this chapter a particular provenance of its own? Ticciati goes on to pursue the idea that in the Dialogue Job mounts a prophetic-style lawsuit against God, the call for a mediator being at the centre of this challenge. Again one can find some verbal parallels with Deut. 28 in parts of the Dialogue (e.g. Deut 28.29/Job 12.25 (5.14); Deut 28.1/Job 17.4; Deut 28.38-40/Job 24.10, 11; 15.33; Deut 28.48, 67/Job 7.4) but are these enough to prove a dependence? In general the kind of model of retributive justice found in the Job Dialogue may show links with a more legalized world-view, but, in my view, links with the wider book of Deuteronomy (excepting chap. 28) itself do not suggest any significant intertextuality. Whilst the Prologue may owe some of its features to this link, in many ways the overall message of the book of Job is a rejection of a narrow view of retributive justice such as might have been associated with a covenantal world-view. It is strange that the covenant model is not otherwise referred to in Job, and that one of its key features is its separation from Israelite concerns. Even Job's lawsuit against God displays a narrower view of reality than in the end he is forced to confront when God appears to broaden Job's horizons. H.H. Rowley (1970) saw the book of Job as essentially reacting against the Deuteronomic retributive model, rejecting a dominant worldview rather than belonging to its radius of influence.

e. *Apocalyptic Elements*

A recent book by Johnson (2009) argues for Job as a nascent apocalypse. Johnson compares the heavenly debate between God and the Satan to a combat myth and he sees the whole book in relation to this model – Job is God's protagonist, his exemplar of the righteous sufferer, and the other characters from his wife to Elihu are all on the Satan's side, trying to undermine Job and make him curse God. So the book is about perseverance in the face of trial. This is a study of genre rather than of intertextual links in that Johnson itemizes aspects of the apocalyptic genre to which Job appears to conform. I would argue that to find apocalypse as an overall genre is taking the argument too far, but he usefully points out some key apocalyptic elements, e.g. 4.12-21 as an apocalyptic vision on the part of Eliphaz, chap. 28 as a revelation and the theophany of Job 38-41 in the same vein. The first of these examples is the best known, seen as "the only vision report by a wise person in Scripture" (W.S. LaSor, D.A. Hubbard and F.W. Bush, 1996: 476). Johnson argues that this vision was originally intended for Eliphaz himself, but he adapts it to refer to Job. Johnson argues for significant indicators of the apocalyptic genre here; "The vision reveals knowledge in the form of a discourse, and while the vision does contain mystical overtones, it does not clearly transport Eliphaz to an 'otherworldly' realm." (Johnson, 2009: 48) Rather there seems to be an otherworldly mediator figure in 4.17-21, although his identification is unclear. So the author is not keeping to a tight script in genre terms – I would argue that this is a deliberate flouting of the wisdom genre rather than a separate apocalyptic genre. Johnson makes the clever point that its being the first element of the first friend's speech is important and this explains why it is Eliphaz, as representative of the three friends, who is specifically rebuked by God in the Epilogue to Job.

Johnson also argues for chap. 28 as a minor theophany, citing verse 23 in particular "God understands the way to it [Wisdom], and he knows its place". Johnson suggests an unidentified mediator in this chapter who imparts also that (v. 28), "the fear of the Lord, that is wisdom". Job as recipient of this revelation arguably begins his most vigorous lament straight afterwards in chap. 29, so Johnson argues that "Job is encouraged and revitalized by the knowledge revealed in chap. 28 that wisdom cannot be found in humans... he thus returns to the 'pre-Dialogue' state of lament over his condition, though he does so with much greater resolve..." (2009: 53). He sees 28.28 as a revelation of knowledge to Job that leads him on to further comprehension and, in the end, salvation and he finds an otherworldly element in the references – to the land of the dead (vv. 13, 22), to hiddenness from the land of the living (v. 21) and to the personified 'deep', all of which, for him, are apocalyptic elements. He finds the listing of precious metals and stones to be in the category of 'revealed secrets' such as one finds in apocalyptic. These kinds of observation are pertinent to the point that even chap. 28, often seen as one of the most 'wisdom' sections of Job, is not exclusively so. The author could alternatively be said to have flouted the wisdom genre here by introducing some apocalyptic elements.

Finally the God speeches are seen by Johnson as a revelation along apocalyptic lines. God takes Job on an otherworldly journey, supported especially
by the speeches of Behemoth and Leviathan as cosmic creatures of chaos
overturned by God. God reveals heavenly secrets which function ultimately to resolve the story in that Job responds and receives enlightenment
through those responses. Theophanic judgement is arguably the tone of the
Yahweh speeches (cf. Perdue, 1991), but Johnson argues that it is Elihu who
is addressed with the opening words of chap. 38, rather than Job, so that
it is the friends who are being judged here, not Job. Admonition to Job is
also present however, for example in 40.2. Johnson's thesis here gives us an
opportunity to see the God speeches in a broader context than simply wisdom and does account particularly well for the 'heavenly' dimension of the
book, as seen in the God speeches and also prologue. These key junctures of
possible influence of a nascent apocalypticism open up more uncertainty as
to the pigeonholing of Job into a narrow wisdom genre and show the author
experimenting with fresh expressions of traditional belief.

These links of Job with a wider thought-world suggest that to restrict Job
to a wisdom classification has tended to narrow our view of Job too much.
It may suggest that such sweeping genre classifications are at the end of the
day unhelpful. However to say that Job is not predominantly a wisdom text
is not to deny that its main discussion of retributive justice springs from
wisdom concerns, although we have seen that even that discussion has a
wider basis in the Israelite thought world. One text that has strengthened
the impression of Job as wisdom is chap. 28, the hymn to wisdom, and it is
to this that I shall now turn to complete this chapter.

7. *Chapter 28 The Hymn to Wisdom*

To end with chap. 28 on wisdom has parallels with the role of the Epilogue
of Job in that the Epilogue seems to confirm the doctrine of retribution that
has just been overturned in the Dialogue. Ending a chapter on wisdom in
which I have argued that Job is essentially not simply wisdom, with a discussion of this text is somewhat ironic! However, I would argue that even
Job 28 has been misunderstood to some extent by being interpreted in the
wisdom category. What is often missed is how different this portrayal of
wisdom is from that in Proverbs and how, once again, it is predominantly
the overturning of traditional ways of looking at things that is the concern
of the author.

This chapter could conceivably be from a different, later 'hand', but
there have been a number of recent studies which have argued convincingly
that it is not necessary to posit a later hand. The purpose of such an addition might be to strengthen the wisdom link of Job, but actually on my

argument I am not denying that there are some wisdom elements in Job and this can be seen as one of them. Perhaps the more knotty literary-critical question is what this speech is doing in the mouth of Job. Is this a separate poem that he is citing, one that had an origin elsewhere? Or is it part of the general dislocation of the third cycle of speeches, meant to be in the mouth of another? Or can it be made sense of in the mouth of Job? Alison Lo has recently argued (2003) that chap. 28 can indeed be regarded as originally Job's and that contradiction is a keynote of the book. She admits that chap. 28 reads more like Zophar's second speech in chap. 11 than the words of Job but argues that Job has a secondary voice alongside his predominant one which allows him to use language and ideas rather like those of the friends. She in fact sees chap. 28 as a transitional chapter drawing a conclusion upon the collapse of the debate between Job and the friends, which has already been hinted at by the drying-up of the friends' speeches. It turns out to be a false conclusion, however, which in turn engages the audience into seeking the real resolution for Job's situation, which is found later in the book. I am not so convinced by this second part of her argument, although I warm to the idea that the chapter can be seen to belong in Job's mouth. Along similar and yet slightly different lines, Claire Egan (2002) argues that chap. 28 makes a pair of chapters with chap. 27. She argues that chap. 28 responds to a preceding speech by Eliphaz in chap. 22. In 22.22 Eliphaz suggests that if Job gives up his wealth to God – expressed in the language of gold, silver and the gold of Ophir – then he will receive God's pleasure. In chap. 28 Job, if he is the speaker as Egan argues, uses the same language of gold, silver and the gold of Ophir to argue that Wisdom cannot be acquired even with such valuable metals. Another key link is the theme of concealment which runs through the third round of speeches (22.12-14; 23.8-9; 24.12-17; 26.9; 27.11) and then is found in chap. 28 where God conceals wisdom from human beings (28.7-11, 13). Egan also finds thematic similarities between chaps. 26 and 28 and argues that when Job appears to contradict himself in these speeches, in comparison to what has gone before, he is often employing a quotation technique, cf. chap. 24. Both of these viewpoints then seek to integrate chap. 28 into the third round of speeches or the structure of the work as a whole. Carol Newsom (2003) sees chap. 28 rather differently as a speculative wisdom poem, separately conceived but original to the work and functioning as a deliberate recasting of the issues of prose tale and wisdom Dialogue. Many scholars see it as integral to the 'plot' of Job, but there are varying evaluations of its originality to Job as a speech. The predominant opinion is that it is an interlude, possibly one that anticipates the speeches of God and it is clear that there are thematic parallels between this chapter and the speeches of God (e.g. verbal parallels between 28.26 and 38.25).

The chapter begins with a description of the way metals are extracted from the earth. Silver mines, the refining of gold, the extraction of iron and the smelting of copper are mentioned in the first two verses and then those who do this work – the miners – are described as tirelessly seeking out the deepest recesses of the earth in order to bring these fine metals to the surface. This then emerges as the theme of this chapter – the quest. The description of the miners continues with their work well away from the rest of humanity, digging deep into the bowels of the earth. The more familiar picture of the earth is as the provider of food, but this is the underside, the hidden depths in which precious stones such as sapphires are found. The places of such treasures are so well hidden, we are told, that even birds of prey, who are used to exploring wild places, and wild animals cannot find them. The miners are the only ones to find these treasures by their dedication to the task. At verse 12 the subject changes from precious metals to wisdom and it is immediately clear that this is the main focus of the passage – the precious metals are ultimately illustrative as a comparison with wisdom. The theme of the elusiveness of wisdom is now played out. Verse 12 asks a rhetorical question – where shall wisdom be found? Wisdom is as elusive as the precious metals. Human beings cannot find it, the seas do not yield it up. In fact, Wisdom is worth more than all these precious metals and stones, above pearls and pure gold. Wisdom is presented here as totally unattainable. The question is repeated in the refrain in verse 20 – where does wisdom come from? The living cannot find it, and even the dead have only heard a rumour of it. The climax comes in verse 23 when it is clear that it is God who understands the way to wisdom because he sees all things and created all things. Wisdom is part of his setting up of the order of the world (cf. Prov. 8.22-30). Another climax comes at the end of the piece (verse 28) where the fear of the Lord is revealed as true wisdom, for to attain wisdom one has to know God and that means departing from evil, i.e. following the doctrine of retribution.

This final verse in its call to depart from evil, does sound a bit like something the friends might say. However, the fear of the Lord is promoted by Job too, particularly in the Prologue but also elsewhere (e.g. Psalm 111.10). In general, unlike Proverbs 8 where wisdom is on offer to human beings to guide them in the ways of life and lead them to God, wisdom here is inaccessible. Perhaps here then too the author of Job is saying something rather contradictory – wisdom is not so readily on offer and in fact is unattainable and unknowable. We are not even sure – apart from rumours – from whence she comes. The imagery is rich in this chapter – the emphasis on gold, silver and other precious metals and stones gives it this richness. The mention of wild beasts anticipates the speeches of God later in the book. The emphasis on the fear of God also sounds a bit like Proverbs 1-9, and it is also the conclusion that Ecclesiastes comes to in the Epilogue, but fearing God, although part of wisdom literature is not solely at home in this genre alone. So the 'hymn to wisdom' is a conundrum – like Job, it seems to spring from wisdom concerns, but it overturns usual ideas and at the end of the day is more of a vehicle for the author to say something rather surprising – i.e. that Wisdom is ultimately inaccessible to humans except through the medium of the divine. I would argue that it does not confirm the book of Job's wisdom credentials, rather it opens up the point that the author, when he was dealing with diverse traditions, had his own particular way of putting a point across and exploring contradictions.

Bibliography

Works Cited

J.F. Priest, 'Humanism, Skepticism and Pessimism in Israel', *JAAR*, 36 (1968), pp. 311-326.

A. Caquot, 'Traits Royaux dans le Personnage de Job' in *Maqqel Shaqedh: La Brance Amander: Hommage a Wilhelm Vischer* (ed. D. Lys, Montpelier: Cause Graille Castelnau, 1960), pp. 32-45.

K.J. Dell, *The Book of Job as Sceptical Literature*, BZAW, 197 (Berlin and New York: Walter de Gruyter, 1991).

K.J. Dell, *Get Wisdom, Get Insight: An Introduction to Israel's Wisdom Literature* (London: Darton, Longman & Todd, 2000).

K.J. Dell, *The Book of Proverbs in Social and Theological Context* (Cambridge: Cambridge University Press, 2006).

M.V. Fox, 'Frame narrative and composition in the book of Qoheleth', *HUCA*, 48, 1977, pp. 83-106.

J.L. Crenshaw, *Old Testament Wisdom: An Introduction* (Louisville, KY: Westminster John Knox Press, 3rd edn, 2010).

D.F. Morgan, *Wisdom in the Old Testament Traditions* (Atlanta: John Knox Press, 1981).

K.J. Dell, '"I will solve my riddle to the music of the lyre' (Psalm XLIX, 4 [5])": A cultic setting for wisdom psalms?' VT LIV/4 (2004), pp. 445-458.

R.N. Whybray, 'Wisdom, Suffering and the Freedom of God in the Book of Job' in *In Search of True Wisdom: Essays in Old Testament Interpretation in Honour of Ronald E. Clements*, JSOTS, 300 (ed. E. Ball, Sheffield: Sheffield Academic Press, 1999), pp. 231-45. Reprinted in *Wisdom: The Collected Works of Norman Whybray* (ed. K.J. Dell and M. Barker, Aldershot: Ashgate, 2005), pp. 194-208.

C. Westermann, *The Structure of the book of Job* (Philadelphia: Fortress Press 1981).

W. Kynes, *'My Psalm Has Turned into Weeping': Job's Dialogue with the Psalms*, BZAW 437, Berlin: Walter de Gruyter, 2012.

L.G. Perdue, *Wisdom and Cult*, SBLDS, 30 (Missoula MA: Scholars Press, 1977).

R.H. Pfeiffer, 'The priority of Job over Is. 40-55', *JBL*, 46 (1927), pp. 202-206.

S. Terrien, 'Quelques Remarques sur les Affinités de Job avec le Deutéro-Ésaïe', *VTS*, 15 (1966), pp. 295-310.

R. Gordis, *The Book of God and Man* (Chicago: University of Chicago Press, 1965).

E. Greenstein, 'Jeremiah as an inspiration to the poet of Job', in *Inspired Speech: Prophecy in the Ancient Near East, Essays in Honor of Herbert B. Huffmon* (ed. J. Kaltner and L. Stulman, London & New York: T & T Clark International, 2004), pp. 98-108.

R. Carroll, *Jeremiah*, Old Testament Guides (Sheffield: JSOT Press, 1989).

M. Weinfeld, *Deuteronomy and the Deuteronomic School* (Oxford: Oxford University Press, 1972).

S. Ticciati, *Job and the Disruption of Identity: Reading beyond Barth* (London: T & T Clark International, 2005).

H. Richter, *Studien zu Hiob* (Berlin: Evangelische Verlagsanstalt, 1959).

B. Gemser, 'The rib or controversy-pattern in Hebrew mentality' in *Wisdom in Israel and in the ANE*, VTS, 3 (ed. M Noth and D W Thomas, Leiden: Brill, 1960), pp. 120-137.

M.B. Dick, 'The legal metaphor in Job 31', *CBQ*, 41 (1979), pp. 37-50.

D. Wolfers, *Deep Things out of Darkness* (Grand Rapids, MI: Eerdmans, 1995).

H.H. Rowley, *Job*, NCB (London: Thomas Nelson and sons, 1970).

T.J. Johnson, *Now My Eye Sees You: Unveiling an Apocalyptic Job* (Sheffield: Sheffield Phoenix Press, 2009).

W.S. LaSor, D.A. Hubbard and F.W. Bush (ed.), *Old Testament Survey: the message, form and background of the Old Testament* (Grand Rapids: Eerdmans, 2nd edn, 1996).

L.G. Perdue, *Wisdom in Revolt* (Sheffield: Almond Press, 1991).

A. Lo, *Job 28 as Rhetoric: An Analysis of Job 28 in the Context of Job 22-31*, VTS, 97 (Leiden and Boston: Brill, 2003).

C. Egan, *The Integrity of Job: a contextual study of Job chapters 24-28*, Unpublished PhD (Birmingham: Birmingham University, 2002).

C.A. Newsom, *The Book of Job: A Contest of Moral Imaginations* (Oxford: Oxford University Press, 2003).

Further Reading

Y. Pyeon, *You have not spoken what is right about me: Intertextuality and the Book of Job*, SBL, 45 (New York: Peter Lang, 2003).

J.L. Crenshaw, 'Wisdom', in *Old Testament Form Criticism* (ed. J. Hayes, San Antonio: Trinity University Press, 1974), pp. 225-264. Reprinted in Crenshaw's *Urgent Advice and Probing Questions* (Macon: Mercer University Press, 1995), pp. 45-77.

L.G. Perdue, 'Wisdom in the Book of Job' in *In Search of Wisdom* (ed. L. G. Perdue, B. B. Scott and W. J. Wiseman, Westminster: John Knox Press, 1993), pp. 73-98.

R. Albertz, 'The Sage and Pious Wisdom in the Book of Job' in *The Sage in Israel and the ancient Near East* (ed.. J. G. Gammie and L. G. Perdue, Winona Lake, IN: Eisenbrauns, 1990), pp. 243-261.

N.C. Habel, 'Of things beyond me: Wisdom in the Book of Job', *CTM*, 10 (1983), pp. 142-154.

3

JOB AS PARODY

1. *Genre Issues*

Finding a key to unlock the book of Job is a tempting exercise which many
have tried to achieve, whether it be a historical, theological or literary key.
My suggestion in this chapter is a literary one, that the author of Job is using
a technique of what in modern parlance we would term parody in order
to convey his at times radical message. Parody can, furthermore, be seen
to illuminate the very structure of the work itself, as suggested in recent
scholarship. However, stressing the importance of parody in this chapter is
not to deny awareness of other keys and other suggestions. We shall see in
Chapter 6 in particular how diverse 'readings' can be. This parody suggestion has its roots in historical-critical discussion however in that it is still
concerned with what effect the author might have been trying to achieve
or what message he was trying to convey.

One of the legacies of form criticism has been to spur an interest in
finding an overall 'genre' for a book. This has led to classification of Job
as a lament (C. Westermann, 1981), a legal Dialogue (W. Richter, 1966),
a diatribe, a tragedy (see Chapter 5), a comedy (J.W. Whedbee, 1977) or
very recently as apocalyptic (T.J. Johnson, 2009). As we saw in the last
chapter these kinds of classification – including the 'wisdom' one – tend
to narrow options rather than broaden them out, and what we find is that
there is truth in all these suggestions, but also a tendency to try to shoe-
horn the whole into one facet of that whole. The book of Job is made up of
many varied genres and that has led some such as D. Wolfers (1995) to say
that in relation to genre, Job is *sui generis*, i.e. it defies genre classification.
Frustration with the question of overall genre has also led some scholars
to try to decide the genre of the book on the basis of the primacy of one
section. For example, M. Cheney (1994) characterizes Job as a frame tale,
seeing the prose sections as the key to interpretation of the book, whilst J.
Course (1994) shows a particular interest in the speeches of Job and the
friends, finding many links between them on grounds of recurrent words
and themes. However this method is ultimately unsatisfactory too. Newsom
(2003) finds a different genre classification for each section (although she
fails to find genres for 29-31 or the Elihu speeches), which is probably closer

to the mark, and argues that it is in the coming together of these genres that Job can be characterized as a 'polyphonic' text. And so I come on to the parody suggestion.

2. *Parody as a Genre*

The parody genre is different from all others because it is not a genre clas-sification in itself, rather it feeds on other genres in order to exist. It is a parasitic genre and there always has to be some pre-existent material for it to parody. The point that the parody makes is generally antithetical to its original, so that it reshapes perception of that original. Parodies can be made using any genre. I would argue that the parody genre usually 'sends up' the original in some way, not necessarily in comic mode; often a comic effect is associated with the definition of parody but I have argued (Dell, 1991) that this is not key to its meaning. Dr. Johnson defined parody as 'a kind of writing in which the words of an author or his thoughts are taken and by a slight change adapted to some new purpose.' In Job's speeches that purpose seems to be to critique traditional positions held by the friends in mocking or sarcastic tone. But that need not be the case for all parodies in all cases. Kynes (2011) puts forward the idea that parodies can be positive rather than simply critical or ironic or with a negative purpose. In order for the reader to appreciate a parody, that reader needs familiarity with the original that is being parodied, so that when it comes to the psalms for example, we can only fully appreciate a parody of either the form or content by knowing the original in reference to a form-critical type in some cases or an actual psalm in others. Sometimes the parody is very subtle and its irony can be lost on an audience. Furthermore, parodies can generate further parodies so that there can be a chain of parodies feeding off an original but also branching out into new thought domains.

3. *Parody as a Technique of the Author of the Dialogue*

My own argument about parody is about critique of known genres by the author of Job on a fairly detailed level, nearly always in the speeches of Job. I will give some salient examples in my key text section. The fact that gen-res from within wisdom but also those outside wisdom circles, in particular psalmic laments and genres from the law court, are featured indicates the broader interaction with the genres of Israelite life by our author. An impor-tant distinction needs to be made here between form, content and context. Sometimes it is essentially the form of a genre that remains the same and so leads to the echo of another text that indicates parody, the Psalm 8 example being a prime one where the form of verse 4 is filled with a new content in a new context in Job 7.17-18 thus creating a parody of the original. The author of the Dialogue wishes to convey that God is an oppressive presence for Job. He therefore conveys this by having Job speak in the very words that would have been used in the Psalms to praise God for his enduring faithfulness to human beings, but in order to convey the opposite of the traditional content. So in Psalm 8.4 the Psalmist says, 'What are human beings that you are mindful of them, mortals that you care for them?' The psalmist expresses awe at the favour God shows to human beings in his creation, and praises his majesty and his name. Job however turns this on its head, 'What are human beings, that you make so much of them, and that you set your mind on them, visit them every morning, test them every moment?' Here God is oppressive to Job who cannot get away. Furthermore, rather than seeing human beings as the apex of God's creative act, as the psalm does, Job rather sees humanity in more mundane terms as 'full of trouble' (14.1).

This is the more common use in Job and conveys the real 'punch' of the author's parody (what I have previously termed the 'misuse of forms'). The reader or audience is expecting a citation or a mild paraphrase, and instead they get a completely overhauled genre, which nevertheless contains enough overtone of the original to be familiar. This is the way the author can convey the parody without losing the sense of the original citation, showing that he takes on board an original meaning and is then deliberately taking it a step further. However, sometimes the form and content may stay the same and it is only the context that is changed (the 'reuse' of forms). This can lead to varying nuances of a citation in new contexts. Another example is when Job pleads for death and longs for a place where he might escape from God: 'O that I might have my request, and that God would grant my desire; that it would please God to crush me, that he would let loose his hand and cut me off! This would be my consolation; I would even exult in pain unsparing; for I have not denied the words of the Holy One.' (6.8-10). Usually in the psalms the desire to flee is from the elements or from other people so that God can more easily be found (Psa. 55.6-8 'And I say, O that I had wings like a dove! I would fly away and be at rest; truly, I would flee far away, I would lodge in the wilderness; I would hurry to find a shelter for myself from the raging wind and tempest.'). Here there are echoes of the lament form with its cry of 'O that' in the Job text, but the content is totally changed.

Actual citation on an intertextual level is also apparent in the Job Dialogue (this Psalm 8 example being the most widely known), which may indicate a deliberate attempt to recall specific texts and play with their ongoing significance and fresh echoes. Where the citation is generally along the lines of the original, the author is interestingly restating a known text in the new context of the mouth of one of the friends or of Job himself. But when the content is substantially changed, usually in the mouth of Job, the author is exploring the fuller implications of the technique of parody. One example is in Job 9.25-8 in relation to Jeremiah's confessions. Instead of finding that he is troubled when he tries to forget God (as Jeremiah was in Jer. 20.9), Job is troubled when he tries to forget his suffering – 'If I say, I will forget my complaint, I will put off my sad countenance, and be of good cheer, I become afraid of all my suffering, for I know that you will not hold me innocent.' (Job 9.27-8) The form of words is very similar to that used in the Jeremiah passage – 'If I say, I will not mention him, or speak any more in my name, then within me there is something like a burning fire shut up in my bones. I am weary with holding it in, and I cannot (Jer. 20.8-9). This looks like more of an intertextual allusion than simply a form-critical paral-lel, although it can be seen in both ways. I would, however, argue then that there are both specific parodies of texts and more generic ones that imitate a well-known genre or idea and that to restrict to one or the other would be to narrow down what the author is doing here.

4. *Parody in the Overall Structure of the Book – Zuckerman's Thesis*

At the same time as my own monograph on Job (1991) another study also brought parody in Job to the fore. We both came to the conclusion, by quite different routes, that parody is the best description of what is going on in Job. Bruce Zuckerman's (1991) view provides support for not only see-ing parody as the description of a technique employed by the author from within the Israelite setting, as I argued, but also views it as an overall clas-sification for the book of Job in relation to extra-biblical parallels. In defini-tion terms, Zuckerman likens parody first to musical counterpoint – a theme played against an original and springing from it and yet subtly varying from it. He writes, 'A parody cannot exist in a literary vacuum: it must have a subject matter that the reader knows quite well, like an often-heard melody or lyric. Only then can a parody act on the reader as it plays its countervail-ing theme over the traditional one.' (1991: 44) He also sees parody as a counterpoint in an oppositional sense, opposing the original theme, twist-ing it inside-out and so denying its validity. He writes, 'Because the parody displays these [traditional] values from a completely different perspective, readers see them with fresh eyes and begin to grasp what is abnormal in the 'normal', what is unconventional about the 'conventional.'" (1991: 44). I termed these authorial uses differently as the 're-use' and 'mis-use' of forms respectively.

As discussed in Chapter 1, scholars have long noted the disharmony between the prose Prologue/Epilogue sections of Job and the Dialogue sec-tion where Job changes from the patient sufferer to the impatient rebel.

I conclude that this juxtaposition of the two sections of Job was a deliberate technique by the author of Job, done with the purpose of throwing up the tension between the possibility of two types of response to suffering – the patient and the impatient (Dell, 1991). Zuckerman however interestingly expresses this idea in the language of parody. He describes the relationship of what he calls the poem of Job to the legend of Job as 'a contrapuntal relationship between a parody and its conventional tradition' (1991: 49) or as a 'parody of Job the Impatient' (1991: 49).

Zuckerman finds three areas of parodistic counterpoint in Job. The first is contained in the proposal that the author of Job in the Dialogue is deliberately amalgamating two existing genres known from the wider ancient Near East together – the Dialogue and the Appeal – focusing on the figure of the righteous sufferer common to each. But he manipulates these genres to serve his own ends, choosing them because of their verbosity. Zuckerman names the Job of the Prologue and Epilogue 'Job the Silent', 'a natural target for the author of the poem to turn inside out' (1991: 97) and make into 'Job the Verbose' in the Dialogue, thus countering the wisdom idea that piety is best exemplified by brevity. Zuckerman notes that the Dialogue/ appeal forms usually represent a personal lament by the sufferer, focusing on their plight. They are used, however, by the author of Job to question God's righteousness in a direct questioning of God. As I have noted in my examples, rather than plead for help Job goes on the attack (9.23-24) and demands justice (13.13-14). Zuckerman also sees the author of Job subverting the conventions of Dialogue with friends – instead of comforting words there is deep conflict. Again, attention is directed away from suffering man and back to the inscrutable God, a God who only ultimately appears in Job because he has been provoked into doing so. Normally in appeal texts godly actions are deemed to speak louder than words, but in Job, the contrary is the case and divine words are far too many.

A second area of parodistic counterpoint located by Zuckerman is the legal metaphor. He notes passages where Job questions the righteousness of God in the role of an offended party in a court case and argues that the author's parody consists in twisting around the normal correspondences in a legal hearing.. He points to 9.2-3 where Job reaffirms his innocence, demands legal recourse and yet despairs of getting it, and longs for an adjudicator. Following M.B. Dick (1979) he sees the legal metaphor in chap. 31 as transforming Job's declaration from a righteous sufferer's appeal into a judicial appeal. He sees Job as trying to divorce God from his role as ultimate legal authority in calling for a mediator figure to judge between them. Thus the conventions of ancient Near Eastern law are dramatically turned on their head. He quotes passages such as 10.2 where Job calls on God to step down from his role of judge and 13.1-2 where Job wants God to give up his power of enforcement so that they can proceed to argue in court as equals. He sees the legal roles of both Job and the friends as reversed – Job becomes plaintiff in 19.6-12, when he tries to prosecute God and the friends are turned into legal antagonists. Zuckermann regards the call by Job for a mediator or arbiter as an appeal to a counter deity. He writes, 'What makes the poet's portrayal of Job's intercessor particularly cutting, from the standpoint of parody, is that it draws upon traditional images of God as champion of the beleaguered and downtrodden and makes them instead the attributes of Job's "counter-god"'(1991: 115). He notes the counterpoint of this with traditional ideas of God as advocate and defender in Jeremiah and Deutero-Isaiah. Then finally when God appears the idea of a counter-deity is squashed – it is clear that there is no Redeemer. This shocks the reader into recognition of the way things really are and the final irony is that the substance of God's speech has nothing to do with the legal merits of Job's case.

The third and final overall parodistic counterpoint found in Job by Zuckerman is what he calls the death theme. Here our work coincides, as Zuckerman points to passages such as 6.2-4, 6.9-10 and 13.17-19 which align with my examples, where the usual desire for relief as found in the Psalms is turned into a desire for death on Job's part. He looks at 3.3-4 and compares it with Jeremiah noting that rather than being a lament of subservience to a divine master as in Jeremiah 20.14-18, it is Job's opening battle cry. He writes of these death-wish passages, 'Ostensibly, they look like standard statements of despair designed to elicit divine pity and help. But they are nothing of the sort... The poet wants his reader ultimately to recognize that things are not meshing together in the conventional pattern.' (1991: 127). Zuckerman sees the hope of resurrection, which he finds in the Epilogue in the giving of the set of new children, as deliberately countered by this death-wish theme in the Dialogue. He sees 14.10-12 for example as making the point that, unlike plants and trees, there is no resurrection hope for humans, death is permanent. He sees the desire to hide in Sheol from God in 14.13-17 as part of the counter-deity theme, but then in 14.18-22 Job wakes from his reverie and sees things as they are.

The advantage of seeing Job in a parodistic way in terms of its overall structure is that parody allows for different genres to be involved and so there is no need to try to fit Job into the straightjacket of one overall genre. As Zuckerman writes, 'If this work is best classified as parody, then the way the Poem turns from type to type, from genre to genre begins to make better sense; for this is the typical method of operation in a parody, that is, the parodist is usually not content to aim his satirical barbs at only one target.' (1991: 136) Whilst I do not agree with all the details of Zuckerman's work, finding particularly unpalatable his idea of a counter-deity and his stress on resurrection themes in the prose story, I think that he has pointed to the wider implication of the use of parody in Job in terms of its overall structure and in comparison with genres of the ancient Near East. Parody suggestions have been taken up by other scholars. Ed Greenstein, for example, comments on the range of techniques employed by the author of Job and includes parody as a key to understanding Job. He writes, 'Sometimes it would seem that the poet of Job makes use of typologies, motifs, images, and phrases that belong to the common stock of ancient Hebrew literature; but at other times it would seem that the Joban poet is drawing on a specific textual source for the purpose of allusion, parody, or elaboration.' (Greenstein 2004: 98)

Parody suggestions have also been made by other scholars. Claire Egan (2002) argues for chap. 28 as a parody of a wisdom speech such as that in Proverbs 8 and a response to elements of the friends' speeches that claim superior access to wisdom. The use of rhetorical questions in vv. 12 and 20 indicates that this is not a simple hymn of praise and they indicate a questioning stance, as do the numerous negations throughout the poem which echo the questions of the Prologue (1.7) and anticipate those of the God speeches. She also notes that 28.28 ironically repeats 1.1, that Job was upright and feared God – the irony is that Job was all those things and yet such qualities have not enabled him to understand his situation through Wisdom. Claus Westermann argued that 'Job 28 admittedly does not correspond at all to the customary wisdom speech.' (1977: 136). He saw the main difference being the inaccessibility of wisdom in this poem whereas in Proverbs, in particular, Wisdom is always there to be acquired (e.g. 4.5). Egan of course sees this hymn as being in Job's mouth against the majority of scholarship. She sees chaps. 9 and 26 also as parodies of creation hymns such as Psalm 104, anticipating the parody of chap. 28. God's reply then responds to Job's parody. Egan writes, 'It is in fact one of the characterizing features of the speeches of God to ask questions, which refer to Job's original argument, but which add nothing new to this in terms of knowledge.' (2002: 154) So, for example, Job's negative assessment in 9.5-7 and 26.7-8 of God's laying the foundations of the earth is picked up in 38.4-7 with a question to Job as to where he was when this foundational act happened. This 'does not, therefore add anything to Job's knowledge, but points to the different perspectives of Job, as a human being, and God' (2002: 154) In chap. 28 God has access to wisdom in a way that human beings do not have. God affirms this in 38.37 for example, 'Who has the wisdom to number the clouds?…' Of course, the inferred answer is that only he does!

The God speeches also show elements of irony. I suggested in my own work that these speeches could perhaps be seen as a parody of set-piece interrogations about the cosmos such as are found in the prophets, e.g. Isa. 40.12-26. In the Isaiah passage the questions are asked by human beings regarding God's creative power and activity and are a means of praising God and extolling his majesty. In Job, the surprise element is that the speeches are by God himself and are designed to quieten human questioning with the answer that God's ways are too mighty for him to understand. In 40.9-14 a hymn of praise is used in a new didactic way to put human beings in their context. The string of rhetorical questions in chap. 38 also conveys a certain sarcasm.

Egan suggests, building on my own suggestions and those of Habel (1985) concerning God's direct response to Job in the God speeches, that in fact chaps. 9 and 26 of the Job Dialogue specifically link up with chaps. 38-39 of God's reply in that they anticipate the way God's answer will be given. In chap. 9 Job predicts that God will appear in a whirlwind and, in the final line of chap. 26, Job's questions predict those by God concerning his power. Given that these chapters of the Dialogue already contain parodies on the theme of creation, the idea of a specific response by God to these parodies would seem to suggest a kind of counter-parody. So in 9.7 Job refers to a God who can command the sun not to rise if he wants to and in 38.12 God asks Job 'Have you commanded the morning?' God echoes Job's accusation in an affirmation that he can indeed do such things! In 9.5-7 God can overthrow the earth's basic structures if he wishes to and in 38.4-7 God confirms that he has indeed constructed the earth according to his own design (see Habel, 1985: 530). In a slightly less convincing example, in 9.16, Job states that God cannot be trusted to answer his cry and in 39.9-12 God gives the wild ox a will that cannot be tamed or trusted by humans (cf. Habel 1985: 532). This seems to me to be more of a lexical echo than an ironic or parodic response. Again in chaps. 9 and 26 Job refers to God's stilling of the sea and killing Rahab and in 38.16 God asks Job if he indeed has 'penetrated the sources of the sea'. In 26.7 the traditional image of solid foundation in the earth appears to be overturned in the idea that the earth and Zaphon are hung over the void. But in 38.1-2 God's reference to solid foundations seems to refute that. In 26.8 God binds up the waters so that 'the cloud is not torn open by them' and in 38.37b-8 this appears to be alluded to in an emphasis on the positive aspects of clouds – i.e. they hold rain and God can control them as he desires. In 26.10 the reference to light and dark having a boundary between them is echoed in 38.19-21 where God asks Job if he knows the way to their dwelling place. The sarcasm contained in all these questions is highly apparent here. In 26.6 Job refers to Sheol and in 38 God asks if he knows about death's secrets. God's response here then turns the parody of traditional creation hymns back into a positive in an ironic response that reverses the parody. God's sarcasm leads to a reversal of Job's former parody leading to a kind of double parodistic counterpoint.

It is my view that parody is a key to the book that still needs to be explored further in the scholarship, and possibly in relation to other biblical books too. Parody is a genre that feeds on other genres and is hence unlike any other genre in its ability to be applied in many and varied contexts.

5. Job's Speeches in the Dialogue

My goal here to give both a taste of the sentiments that Job expresses and a sense of how the author conveys Job's scepticism towards the traditional arguments being proferred by the friends in his use of the parody technique. I shall ascribe the parody to the character of Job in what follows, but, of course, the author's intention lies behind the portrayal.

Round One

The opening chapter of the Dialogue featuring the 'impatient' Job is a heart-rending lament. He curses the day of his birth in wishing that the day had never happened, wishing it a day of darkness, of night, of non-existence in the calendar. That particular night too is to be cursed and should not see the morning light. In an opening parody of Jeremiah's similar confession that wishes he too had never been born (Jer 20.14-18), Job also wishes that he had never been conceived and so curses the night of his conception. He depersonalizes those who attended the birth (described in Jeremiah as his mother, father and a messenger) with questions about why there were 'knees to receive me' (v. 12) which could refer to father or mother, 'womb' (v. 11) and 'breasts for me to suck' (v. 12) (perhaps an indirect reference to his mother but not a very fulsome one) and the personified night that announced his birth (v. 3). Job's intensification of Jeremiah's curse (which may indeed have been a more widespread known form) with parodic effect relays the level of his grief and despair. Job wishes he had died at birth for death is a release for all, small or great. A sense of death as the great level-ler comes in here. This longing for death parodies more traditional lament sentiments that ask God to deliver the sufferer from death (e.g. Psa. 88.4-5 sees death as undesirable). Job asks about the irony of why people who long for death such as him are instead given life. He describes God as having fenced him in so that he cannot find his own way. He describes his sighing as being so integral to him that it is like his bread and water. He had dreaded this kind of trouble coming upon him – presumably that was why he was so scrupulous about his sacrifices – and here it is! This is indeed a very differ-ent portrayal of Job from the accepting figure of the Prologue. It represents introduction of a 'real' character by the author, one who comes immedi-ately to life in this opening soliloquy. Ostensibly this speech is addressed to the friends who immediately reply, although it has the tone of someone lamenting to God and the world without the air of direct address that we find later in the Dialogue.

After Eliphaz's reply, Job 'answers' in chaps. 6 and 7. These chapters are a continuing bewailing of his condition. He feels the heaviness of his burden of calamity and blames God for having sent his 'terrors' against him. He longs for death at this point, feeling worn and energyless. He parodies sentiments that long to get away from the human situation to be with God (e.g. Psa. 55.6-8), saying rather that he longs to get away from God's oppressive treatment of him. He reiterates that 'I have not denied the words of the Holy One' (v. 10), maintaining his innocence of wrongdoing. There is a barbed comment probably directed at the friends in 6.14 about the wrongness of withholding 'kindness from a friend'. This is followed by a description of his companions as being as treacherous as a fast flowing icy torrent, which melts in summer and causes those who rely on the water's sustenance to perish. To this he likens the friends who came to see one thing – the old Job presumably – and have found another. He accuses them of being afraid of his calamity, he who has asked nothing of them in monetary terms. In 6.24-30 he challenges the friends directly to tell him where he has gone wrong. At the start of chap. 7 Job bewails the human condition and describes the emptiness of his life, day and night. His nights are long and sleepless and his days slip by too quickly. For the first time he complains about his skin disease here (v. 5). He dwells on the brevity of life and the finality of death, reflecting the belief of the time that the dead went to Sheol, a land from which they could not return. He needs to speak out and he feels God's oppressive presence. In his parody of Psa. 8.4 he longs to escape from God's presence and wonders why God is so overly-concerned with humans that he cannot leave them alone! Job feels that death is close, soon it will be too late for God to pardon him – God will seek Job and find him gone.

Bildad, the second friend, now has a chance to reply and Job then answers in chaps. 9-10 – note that Job gets longer speeches than the friends, possibly reflecting the author's sympathy for Job's position. Job raises the general question – how can a mortal be just before God? The issue is God's greatness which makes it impossible to contend with such a mighty power. What appears to be a description of God's creative power in vv. 5-10 proves to be a clever parody of just those kinds of description that usually praise God's works in creation (e.g. Psa. 104). Here, however, his acts are seen to be negative ones, just showing his power and anger rather than his beneficence. There is no one who can question his acts or hold him to account. Such is God's power and anger that what chance has Job in persuading God of his innocence? Such is God's might that he wouldn't even listen to

Job. Job reiterates his blamelessness and self-loathing accompanied by his helplessness in the face of the all powerful. He decides in v. 22 that God destroys both blameless and wicked – the doctrine of just retribution is not working and God allows wickedness to flourish in the earth. In the last part of chap. 9 Job parodies Jer. 20.8-9 using very similar phrases when he says that he is troubled when he tries to forget his suffering knowing that God is condemning him. Jeremiah on the other hand is troubled when he tries to forget God. In chap. 10 instead of the all-seeing eye of God being praised as in the Psalms (e.g. Psalm 139.7-8), Job complains that he cannot get away from God who 'contends against me' God is everywhere, as creator he knows everything about his created beings. Again the description of God's creation of a human being in vv. 8-12 sounds like a hymn of praise (particularly akin to Psalm 139.13-16), but is in fact its opposite. For example, 10.11 'You clothed me with skin and flesh, and knit me together with bones and sinews' strongly recalls Psa. 139.13 with similar vocabulary used, 'For it was you who formed my inward parts; you knit me together in my mother's womb' and yet the context of Job is an accusation of present destruction (v. 8) and self-loathing (v. 1) whilst the psalmic verse is in the context of pure praise. The real purpose of all this was to keep control of Job, to keep watch and seek him out. In a parody of passages that long for God, Job begs to be left alone. He asks again why God allowed him even to be born – given that mistake, can't he be left alone to live out his short number of days in peace?

It is now the turn of Zophar, the third friend, to reply and he instills a direct response from Job at the beginning of chap. 12. Job states that he is not inferior in his understanding to them – he knew all the old arguments, but his experience has changed everything. He sees that he is being laughed at by his friends for having been so God-fearing and for now having fallen on hard times. The wicked again seem to be prospering at the expense of the good. In vv. 7-9 there is a surprising call upon the animals and birds who can teach human beings a thing or two – the natural world witnesses to God's activity. Here, though, Job is saying it is all upside-down – yes God has ultimate power but he is not using it in the right way to reward wisdom and good behaviour. So he parodies the traditional line that nature witnesses to the glory of God (e.g. Psa. 98.7-9) by seeing God's actions as negative. Again he reiterates God's power, but sees it as destructive, reversing positive praise of God's power as in Psalms such as 107 (see Job 12.21, 24 cf. Psa. 107.40). God is seen to work against human beings – God makes fools of counsellors, judges, kings and priests so that the mighty are fallen at his hand. God does it because God can, not because of any moral imperative.

In chap. 13 Job challenges God to an argument. He jibes at the friends and wishes they would keep quiet. He accuses them of speaking falsely for

God. In the face of God's power nothing can be kept secret and his power will simply overwhelm them. These are the words of an increasingly desperate man. Job says that even if God tries to kill him, he will still defend himself. Job holds on to God – he is beginning to speak in the language of the law court about his 'case', 'defending his ways', 'my declaration', 'vindication'. His plea is still to be left alone, but failing that he wants a chance for a hearing. He wants to know what he has done wrong. In a parody of psalms that long to see God's face (e.g. Psalm 27.4), Job hides himself from God's face and asks for God's hand to be withdrawn. But then in contradictory fashion he asks why God is hiding his face and treating Job as an enemy – God is not being honest and open with him.

Job's assessment of humanity in chap. 14 is as 'full of trouble'. His life is fleeting – why then does God take so much trouble over him? Again God is an oppressive presence for him and for humanity at large and he pleads for God to leave human beings to get on with life. This parodies passages in the psalms (e.g. Psalm 55) where the psalmist wants to escape from enemies not from God. In this chapter Job goes on to talk about trees and stumps and the way that they recover, comparing that to humans for whom death is a one-way ticket. This starts to worry him as it would mean the end of his argument with God or of his chance for vindication. So in verse 13 he changes his plea from death to a temporary concealment in Sheol whilst God is still angry. Once God's anger had abated Job would be there to be back in relationship with God. This leads him to a positive moment of thinking of what a good relationship with God again would look like. Then comes the 'But' in verse 18 – just as God destroys mountains, rocks, stones and soil and so ultimately the earth itself, so God destroys human hopes by wearing them away. In contrast to psalms which hope for good things because of trust in God (e.g. Psa. 28.6-8) Job accuses God of deliberately destroying the hopes of those who trusted God and of lying them low, as in Job's own case. Much of this generalizing on Job's part has a direct relevance to his own situation. It is interesting how he changes his arguments and seems to come at the same problem from different angles. He has mood swings from negative, to angry, to positive, all signs of a person suffering intensely, both physically and psychologically. And so we reach the end of the first cycle of speeches and it is about to begin all over again in round two.

Round Two

Job begins his second round in chap. 16 with an attack on the friends, accusing them of talking too much and imagining their roles reversed in which case he could condemn them, or provide encouragement, as he chose.

By contrast, if he speaks in his present state it doesn't ease his suffering. He then turns his attack onto God whom he sees as to blame for his suffering and who has become his enemy. Usually God is perceived to give people the strength to go on even in the face of difficult times (e.g. Psalm 94.18-19). Job, however, in parodying mode, accuses God of having worn him out, shriveled him up, torn him apart and gnashed his teeth against him, to name but a few of the accusations. There follows a bitter description of God's attack on him, using the ungodly as his agents. Despite Job's penitence and innocence, this is his fate. Chapter 16 ends with a lament from Job that he should not die, but rather his cry of innocence will ever ring out. He realizes that God is his only witness, even though God has seemingly let him down. He cries out to that God for justice nevertheless. In chap. 17 Job appears to hit a new 'low'. He feels that he is near to death. He chides the friends to side with him. In verse 6 he is back to chastising God. He is feeling sorry for himself and describes his ever worsening physical state. He sees the friends as behaving like the self-righteous innocent, condemning him as godless, when in fact he can see that they have got it all wrong. Job feels trapped – he cannot escape from his distress or from God. If he looks to death, then he has no hope of continuing to justify himself to God. He asks rhetorically whether hope will go down to Sheol with him, expecting the answer 'no'. There is an echo of Psalm 139 here in the mention of Sheol – this Psalm asserts that in heaven or in Sheol God is there (vv. 8, 11, 12) and views the all-seeing eye of God as a good thing (vv. 14-15). Job on the other hand is not so assured that Sheol is a good option!

Chapter 19 begins the second response – this time to Bildad whom Job accuses of tormenting him with words. Job continues to maintain his innocence and his sense of being closed in by God's net, or his path blocked by a wall and obscured by darkness. He accuses God of attacking him using rich imagery of an uprooted tree and besieging armies. He goes on to the point that other people are estranged from him, such that even his own servants won't answer him. His illness has made him repulsive even to his wife. Everyone is against him and his body is thin and emaciated. He accuses the friends of hounding him, just as God has. In verse 21 Job changes his tone and wishes that he could write down his words in a permanent way to ensure that his innocence is recorded for posterity. He then brings in the idea of a Redeemer. Is this a third party who might judge between him and God or is he simply calling God 'redeemer' in the hope that at some point God will vindicate him? Much scholarly ink has been spilled over this passage. When Job talks about seeing God is it whilst he is still alive, even though his skin is 'destroyed' presumably by illness, or does he mean after his skin has decayed and he is dead, i.e. that after death he will be vindicated? Translation issues are involved here. My own preference is not to take this passage as evidence of belief in an afterlife but rather to see Job as expressing a hope that a miraculous change in God will mean that he is vindicated at some point. Whether the 'redeemer' is a third party – that is possible, although it might be a hypothetical thought and hope on Job's part.

Job's response to the third friend, Zophar, begins in chap. 21. He begs to get a word in edgeways. He justifies his complaining tone and then goes on to bewail the seeming prosperity of the wicked which goes against the grain of the usual doctrine of just retribution. The wicked don't even want to know God and see their achievements as their own. This passage both parodies passages which discuss the prosperity of the righteous and those that discuss the prosperity of the wicked but in negative terms. In Psalm 73 the prosperity of the wicked is described but in a negative way – here Job describes wholly positive things happening to them. In Psalm 73 the prosperity of the wicked is only temporary and by the end of the psalm the wrong is righted, but in Job there is no suggestion of the situation being rectified. From verse 17 Job asks a series of rhetorical questions expecting the answer 'never'. Never do bad things happen to wicked people! He cites the friends as saying that the next generation will suffer in their place, but he calls for the need for them to be punished. He sees death as the great leveller that means that the prosperous lie down in the grave along with the embittered. The whole chapter concerns this theme of the sparing of the wicked and the lack of punishment of them – they are never reproached. He reveals that he is not convinced by the arguments of the friends or their consolations.

Round Three

Eliphaz starts up again in chap. 22 and then is responded to by Job in 23. Job is having a bad day! He longs to find God so that he can lay out his arguments before him. He imagines listening to God's reply, learning and understanding and God in turn listening to him – that is the kind of Dialogue he would like – and his acquittal would be automatic. By contrast, he cannot find God. There is an interesting change of mood here – earlier on Job could not get away from God and found his presence oppressive (e.g. chaps. 13-14). Now he complains that God is absent – he cannot see him. This contrasts with psalms such as 23 where God's presence is constant (Job 23.8-9 cf. Psalm 139.8-10). In verse 10 Job expresses the view that this might be a test from which he will emerge like gold. He reasserts his righteous behaviour. He also expresses the realization that God does what he likes and has a plan for him. He finishes his speech expressing his terror at God's might and his desire to vanish into darkness. In chap. 24, Job describes the wrongdoing of the wicked and asks again about God's accountability – God seems to do nothing in the face of these immoral acts. God does not seem to hear the prayer of the helpless victims of their misdeeds (verse 12). Job now describes the deeds of the wicked in more negative terms, associating acts of murder and adultery with darkness and night time.

Scholars often wonder what vv. 18-20 are doing in the mouth of Job because suddenly he seems to contradict himself and say that the wicked are punished by a one-way ticket to Sheol and by the lack of any remembrance of them. Traditionally these verses have been reassigned to chap. 25, Bildad's third and uncharacteristically short speech. Perhaps there is some scribal error here. Another alternative is that the author is trying to convey the confusion of Job's mind and thus have him contradict himself on this subject of the wicked. The other remaining verses of chap. 24 have also sometimes been seen as not Job's own, although the sentiments seem at home in Job's mouth in my view. Verse 21 links up with vv. 1-12; in vv. 22-4 Job may simply be describing the mighty (subtly different from the wicked) and the security God gives them before they are brought low. It is not clear here whether Job thinks the mighty are good or bad and hence whether their demise is simply the natural way of things or some kind of punishment. Verse 25 is in line with his usual challenges to the friends.

In contrast to Bildad's short speech in chap. 25, Job seems to pick up his momentum again in chaps. 26 and 27. We have no third speech from Zophar and again some dislocation of verses that are now in the mouth of Job may have taken place. Job's speech begins with a sarcastic tone, seemingly addressed to the friends, although it could be to God. Certainly from verse 5 his words describe God's power, which is the theme of the rest of the chapter. Unlike such descriptions however, Job here stresses the frightening nature of God's power, more than is usual in such proclamations. There is a marked contrast with the usually praiseworthy tone of hymns to God's power such as in Isaiah 40.9-11. In chap. 27 Job bewails his own situation again and maintains his innocence in the face of God's hostility. He pleads in verse 7 that his enemy – presumably God, or at least the friends – be like the wicked and hence punished. Verses 8-10 seem to continue this thought, although they contradict his usual line about the wicked not being properly punished. In verse 11 Job claims that he knows about God and can teach about God's ways to others. Some scholars think that vv. 8-11 of this chapter are part of the lost third speech of Zophar and so it is he who is maintaining traditional views about the wicked and teaching Job about God. This is a possibility, but these sentiments could also belong with Job himself. Perhaps this uncertainty about who is saying what at this point is one of the author's deliberate techniques rather than any failure in the structure of the book or as a result of scribal transmission. Verse 12 seems to refer to the vanity of the friends in Job's eyes – if it is in the mouth of

Zophar it would read as a more general statement about those who have trodden the path of wisdom. When we get to verse 13, there is more consensus about this being from Zophar since it is a traditional position on the punishment of the wicked that is being represented. However there are none of the opening and closing jibes that are usually present. The rest of the chapter pursues this theme.

Job's Closing Soliloquy

Chapters 29-31 represent Job's closing soliloquy, matching his opening one in chap. 3. Job begins by recalling the good days, when God was with him, when he was respected by society, when he did good works, when he saw the future in a rosy hue, when his words were valued by others and when he had kingly authority over others. This chapter is so overstated that it has possible overtones of a parody of royal descriptions of kings. The idea of nobles refraining from speech and princes being hushed (vv. 9-10) sounds almost comic in reference to Job himself but might have been the kind of description that would have been common of kings. This is in contrast to Job's miserable present which is described in chap. 30. The young taunt him, even those at the margins of society, such as the children of the wicked. They persecute and terrorize Job and no one tries to stop them. In verse 16 Job goes back to the topic of his illness and blames God for it all again. He wants to have a conversation with God, but he is ignored. He accuses God of turning cruel and persecuting him and he worries again about the inevitability of death. He tries to reason with God – surely God does not ignore those who cry for assistance. He recalls again how, in his prosperous days, he was there for the needy. He bewails his lot over and over again – his illness and his mourning make him a pathetic figure. In chap. 31, Job is in slightly more defiant mode again. He could be parodying the kind of legal metaphor that asks 'if…then' in particular cases – here the kind of detail he goes into is more personal than ever would be tried in a lawcourt and in that lies the disjunction, for example in vv. 26-8, 'If I have looked at the sun when it shone, or the moon moving in splendour, and my heart has been secretly enticed, and my mouth has kissed my hand, this also would be an iniquity.' He wants to reassert that immoral actions should be punished and that God sees all and acts accordingly, but these kinds of action could never really be recognized as immoral. He asks that if he has sinned then punishment should be his, but with the inference that he knows that he hasn't sinned and so this punishment is unjust, hence there is strong irony here. This is also a kind of reversal of the good deeds enumerated in chap. 29. At the end of the chapter he longs for someone to hear him. He longs for an accusation to which he can respond and justify himself. He is a desperate man at this stage, crying out for vindication from God. He is the defendant against God the attacker in a parody of the usual pattern where God is the defendant against human beings who attack, e.g. Micah 6.3-5. The words of Job then come to an end and, with them, the Dialogue. The parody of the author has come through time and time again in the overturning of traditional sentiments by Job which in turn conveys his intense emotion, despair, anger and grief. This parody is the genius of the Job poet.

Bibliography

C. Westermann, *The Structure of the Book of Job* (Philadelphia: Fortress Press, 1981).

W. Richter, *Recht und Ethos: Versuch einer Ortung des Weisheitlichen Mahnspruches* (München: Kösel Verlag, 1966).

J.W. Whedbee, 'The Comedy of Job', *Semeia* 7 (eds. R. Polzin and D. Robertson, Missoula: Scholars Press, 1977), pp. 1-39.

T.J. Johnson, *Now my Eye Sees You: Unveiling an Apocalyptic Job* (Sheffield: Sheffield Phoenix Press, 2009).

D. Wolfers, *Deep Things out of Darkness: The Book of Job, Essays and a New English Translation* (Grand Rapids, MI: Eerdmans, 1995).

M. Cheney, *Dust, Wind and Agony: Character, speech and genre in Job* (CB, 36, Stockholm: Almqvist & Wiksell, 1994).

J.E. Course, *Speech and Response: A Rhetorical Analysis of the Introductions to the Speeches of the Book of Job (Chaps 4-24)*, CBQMS, 25 (Washington DC: Catholic Biblical Association of America, 1994).

C.A. Newsom, *The Book of Job: A Contest of Moral Imaginations* (Oxford: Oxford University Press, 2003).

K.J. Dell, *The Book of Job as Sceptical Literature*, BZAW, 197 (Berlin and New York: Walter de Gruyter, 1991).

W. Kynes, 'Beat Your Parodies into Swords, and Your Parodied Books into Spears: A New Paradigm for Parody in the Hebrew Bible', *Biblical Interpretation* 19 (2011) pp. 276-300.

B. Zuckermann, *Job the Silent: A Study in Historical Counterpoint* (Oxford: Oxford University Press, 1991).

M.B. Dick, 'The legal metaphor in Job 31', *CBQ,* 41 (1979), pp. 37-50.

E. Greenstein, 'Jeremiah as an inspiration to the poet of Job' in *Inspired Speech: Prophecy in the Ancient Near East, essays in Honor of Herbert B. Huffman* (eds. J. Kaltner and L. Stulman, London & New York: T & T Clark International, 2004), pp. 98-108.

C. Egan, *The Integrity of Job: a contextual study of Job chapters 24-28*, Unpublished PhD (Birmingham: Birmingham University, 2002).

N.C. Habel, *The Book of Job*, OTL (London: SCM Press, 1985).

Further Reading

T.N.D. Mettinger, 'Intertextuality: Allusion and Vertical Context Systems in Some Job Passages' in eds. H. McKay and D.J.A. Clines, *Of Prophets' Visions and the Wisdom of Sages*, JSOTS, 162 (Sheffield: JSOT, 1993).

M. Fishbane, 'The Book of Job and Inner-Biblical Discourse' in *The Voice from the Whirlwind* (eds L.G. Perdue and W.C. Gilpin, Nashville TN: Abingdon Press, 1992).

M. Fishbane (ed.), *Reading Between Texts: Intertextuality and the Hebrew Bible* (Literary Currents in Biblical Interpretation, Louisville KY: Westminster/John Knox Press, 1992).

E.M. Good, *Irony in the Old Testament* (London: SPCK, 1965).

4

JOB IN THE CONTEXT OF THE ANCIENT NEAR EASTERN WORLD

The book of Job seems to have its closest counterparts from the ancient Near Eastern world in Mesopotamian material from ancient Sumer and Babylon, although there are also minor Egyptian and Ugaritic works of parallel interest. It is curious that whilst Proverbs has the closest connection with Egypt, particularly in the similarity of the instruction genre, Job's parallels are from a different culture altogether, mainly the Babylonian which took over from the very ancient Sumerian culture. This might add more fuel to the argument that these books spring from very different thought-worlds. Suffering and complaint do not appear to have been particularly on the Egyptian agenda, whilst in Mesopotamia such concerns seem to be primary, and this material closely resembles lament forms.

Amongst Egyptian material, the *Satirical Letter of the Scribe Hori*, a satire about a pompous and pretentious scribe who sarcastically questioned a pupil on the geography of the region, has a slight similarity to Job in its use of rhetorical questions in the God speeches (see G. Von Rad, 1966). We also find from Egypt some more pessimistic texts that bewail the decadence of society and its moral decay, for example *The Admonitions of Ipuwer*, a piece which describes a chaotic time in which people long for death and God cannot be found. It is, however, often social injustice rather than a questioning of divine justice that is of concern. There are also some more individualistic texts, such as *The Dispute of a Man with his Soul* in which death is longed for (and suicide contemplated) by the sufferer, but then his soul rebukes him and recommends hedonistic pleasure instead. This perhaps resembles the biblical book of Ecclesiastes rather than Job. It is clear that the problem of theodicy – i.e. the justice (or not) of God – does not seem to have been a major preoccupation in Egypt. An Ugaritic text on the theme of theodicy, that may owe its provenance to familiarity with the Mesopotamian works I mention below, has been found at Ugarit (RS 25.460 in Ugaritica V, Paris, 1968, 264-73, cited by Day (1995)). This suggests that the righteous sufferer theme was known early on in Canaan, thus suggesting possible local influence on Job.

Apart from the Ugaritic material, these ancient Near Eastern parallels are up to a thousand years or more apart historically from the biblical

material. Scholars have tried to extrapolate contextual conclusions from one
to the other, but actually this is hard to prove. Whilst we know that texts
were copied by scribes for the purposes of learning to read and write and for
archival functions and that there were libraries of key texts in the ancient
world, we do not know, more specifically, how the particular Job parallels
were preserved and transmitted. It is hard to evaluate actual dependence of
one text upon another. It is more likely that it was the thought-world that
was the source of influence upon the Job author. He may have been familiar
with famous texts from the Mesopotamian world if he was an educated
person. However, rather than trying to recreate unproveable historical links
perhaps it is more interesting and productive in this chapter to look at the
literary and theological links to be found between texts.

1. *Ancient Sumerian Wisdom*

The Sumerian culture is the oldest in the world, with many of their key
texts formulated according to their own system of writing by circa 2500 BCE
(S.N. Kramer, 1952). Excavations at Nippur have revealed a possible scribal
quarter and we have tablets dating from the second millennium BCE that
indicate that education went on there. There were Edubba or Tablet Houses
where education took place for those destined for high positions in society
and so tablets were copied, recited and archived in such circles. On such a
cuneiform tablet we find a Sumerian text close in sentiment to the biblical
book of Job – *Man and his God*. This is a hundred and forty line poem in
monologue form probably from the beginning of the second millennium BCE.
It is a lament prompted by both misfortune and sickness and is hence very
close to Job's situation where he is first struck with misfortune and then
with an unpleasant skin disease. In the Sumerian parallel the idea that such
misfortune may be the result of sin is aired but in the more universal context
of the sinfulness of humanity as a race. The gods are not blamed here. There
is a similar lamenting tone from the author, but the conclusion is that it is
better to remain faithful to one's god and pray for a change of circumstance.
This duly occurs and, like Job, there is a happy ending to this tale in which
the sufferer is delivered from his misfortune. The individual nature of this
piece and airing of both lament and ultimate restoration makes this a significant parallel to Job. The sufferer is an individual with fidelity to his own god
even within a polytheistic milieu. All that is lacking is the sense of outrage
and protest that the biblical Job utters in the Dialogue.

  Man and his God begins with a didactic exhortation on the need to praise
one's god. The sufferer complains that the 'man of deceit' has taken him
over (line 30; cf. Job 16.9-11 in which God has turned into Job's adver-
sary and the wicked overpower him). The sufferer is overcome with various

diseases and he cannot even fulfil the practical aim of being able to eat. His lament is bitter and long. He complains of ill-treatment by others (friends twist his words in line 38; cf. Job 6.15-21 where friends have turned treacherous), of depression and physical illness (line 47, cf. Job's complaint of short days in 7.4-6 and 9.25, and destiny for a life of pain in 14.22) and he muses that mortal man has never been perfect (line 105, cf. Job 4.17-18 where Eliphaz asks, 'Can mortals be righteous before God?'). He makes a public declaration of his sin in line 115, something Job refuses to acknowledge, although Job asks, in 13.23, 'How many are my sins?' The sufferer stresses the need for his family and friends to lament on his behalf, a theme lacking in our biblical book – rather, for Job, he is repulsive to his wife and others (19.14-17). There is a continuing sense of homage throughout however with the Sumerian sufferer's confession of sin and plea for mercy and restoration. The outcome is that his prayer is accepted and he is restored to health (cf. the epilogue in 42.7-17 where Job's restoration to good health is assumed but not stated alongside his restoration to prosperity). A prayer of thanksgiving ends the piece, something we do not find in Job, partly because the Epilogue is in prose rather than in poetry.

So there are instructive parallels here on quite a detailed level with striking thematic similarities with Job's own sentiments. This indicates a shared experience of suffering and reaction to it across the cultures rather than an actual textual dependence, although the fact that this Sumerian text went on to be preserved in Babylonian circles that also produced such texts indicates that cross-cultural interchange was likely. It is to the Babylonian parallels, which are more extensive, that I shall now turn.

2. Babylonian Parallels

Although there are significant parallels to Job in Babylonian material, it is interesting that there was no nomenclature of 'wisdom' in Babylonian circles. W.G. Lambert writes in his book, *Babylonian Wisdom Literature* that:

"Wisdom" is strictly a misnomer as applied to Babylonian literature ... Though this term is thus foreign to ancient Mesopotamia, it has been used for a group of texts which correspond in subject-matter with the Hebrew wisdom books' (Lambert 1960: 1).

It is primarily as lament that this Babylonian material forms a parallel to Job (see Gray, 1970), and this is worth noting in relation to our previous discussion of Job's genre in chap. 2. Perhaps this reinforces the argument for Job as existing outside the main Israelite wisdom corpus, closer perhaps to lament literature as a genre. Lambert also notes that there is a point of change between the Sumerian outlook and that of the Babylonian that led to the issue of the gods' justice being raised that very much characterizes the literature of the later nation. He points out that the gods were originally perceived as simply personifications of aspects of nature who basically had the freedom to act as they liked ostensibly within nature's boundaries, but sometimes broke outside those boundaries when storms and earthquakes occurred. However, at a more mature stage of thought, human beings tried to impose a human-centred purpose on both the human and divine worlds and this was a cause of tension. When the gods then did not behave as human beings would expect or like, it led to questions being raised about their nature and power. Lambert writes, 'The big problem in Babylonian thought was that of justice. If the great gods in council controlled the universe, and if they ruled it in justice, why ...?' (Lambert, 1960: 10). Human justice did not seem to be matched on the divine plane.

This is why the main parallels to Job are found in Babylonian material, because of the questioning of the gods that emerges as situations of suffering lead to a challenge to the gods' justice. For example, the Babylonian *Dialogue between a man and his god* treats the problem of theodicy in the face of undeserved suffering. It features an innocent man, similar to Job, saying, 'The wrong I did I do not know' (section ii). Thus rather than there being a confession of sin as in the Sumerian parallel, knowledge of any sin is explicitly denied as in Job (9.20-21; 13.23). Suffering in the form of illness is assumed in this work, as in biblical wisdom literature, to be punishment for sin. Likewise restoration to health again is a sign of divine favour. The first half of this Dialogue features the sufferer, the second half, his god. So in section ix the god states 'the gate of life and well-being is open to you!' (cf. Job 38.17 where God speaks to Job).

The main parallels to the book of Job are the *Ludlul bel nemeqi* – *I will praise the Lord of Wisdom* – and the *Babylonian Theodicy*, both from between 1500 and 1200 BCE and both treating the problem of the failure of the piety-equals-prosperity nexus. Let us focus on the parallels of these with Job.

a. *LUDLUL BEL NEMEQI (The Babylonian Job)*

Like the Sumerian *Man and his God*, *Ludlul* is a monologue rather than a Dialogue. The sufferer questions his suffering from disease and at the hands of others asking why Marduk, his god, allows it to happen. This sufferer, like Job, was a model of piety and an authority figure in the community but is now despised from his god down to the king and to his slaves. He sees the gods as having caused his disease, treating him as a wrongdoer when he was not one. This story too has a happy ending in that the sufferer is eventually restored to health and fortune, following three dreams, in which different characters appear, which begin the process of the subsidence of Marduk's wrath.

There were originally four tablets, but the state of preservation of the material is incomplete. The beginning and end of the first tablet is missing, the second is complete, the third is mainly complete, the fourth is fragmentary. The loss of the beginning of the first tablet makes it unclear who is speaking. The opening lines 'I will praise the lord of wisdom' indicate that the sufferer is addressing Marduk, the head of the Babylonian pantheon. There are three names mentioned in tablet three of people of high standing – Laluralimma, Urnindinlugga, and Subsi-mesre-Sakkan – and it could be one of these – probably the last – who is speaking here and who may even be the author.

Let us take a closer look at each of the tablets and their similarities with the biblical book of Job. I have put lines from each in parallel to show the similarity. Tablet 1 deals with the complainant's suffering at the hands of the gods and other people, including his own family. It also describes the bodily effects of his grieving.

Ludlul 1. 43 – My god has forsaken me and disappeared.

Job 13.24 – Why do you hide your face, and count me as your enemy?

Ludlul 1. 47 – My strength is gone; my appearance has become gloomy.

Job 16.7-8a – Surely now God has worn me out; he has made desolate all my company. And he has shrivelled me up.

Ludlul 1. 48 – My dignity has flown away, my protection made off.

Job 19.9 – He has stripped my glory from me, and taken the crown from my head.

Ludlul 1. 54 – When I lie down at night, my dream is terrifying.

Job 7.4 – When I lie down I say, 'When shall I rise?'

But the night is long, and I am full of tossing until dawn.

Job 7.13-14 – When I say, 'My bed will comfort me, my couch will ease my complaint.' Then you scare me with dreams and terrify me with visions.

Ludlul 1. 92 – My family treat me as an alien.

Job 19.13 – He has put my family far from me,

And my acquaintances are wholly estranged from me.

Ludlul 1. 98 – I have no one to go at my side, nor have I found a helper.

Job 30.13 – They break up my path, they promote my calamity;

No one restrains them ['they have no helper' in some translations].

Ludlul 1. 105 – By day there is sighing, by night lamentation.

Job 3.24 – For my sighing comes like my bread, and my groanings are poured out like water. Truly the thing that I fear comes upon me.

Ludlul 1. 109 – My eyes...[through] constant weeping
110 My lower eyelids are distended [through abundance of] tears.
Job 16.16 – My face is red with weeping, and deep darkness is on my eyelids.
Job 16.20b – My eye pours out tears to God.
Job 17.7 – My eye has grown dim from grief, and all my members are like a
   shadow.

Tablet 2 attributes this suffering to the gods and bewails the useless attempts
at exorcism by the priests in an interesting cultic twist. It then considers the
ethical problem of the suffering of the righteous. The sufferer lists his past
pieties and complains that he is being treated as a wrongdoer. He complains
that the divine world does not appear to work according to human rules.
This opens up the wider issue of the uncertainty of human existence. He
complains at length about his disease, seen in terms of evil spirits, which no
priestly incantation can overcome and which, it seems, the gods are powerless to counter. He also complains that others exploit his downfall to their
own advantage. At the end of this tablet there is an upbeat confession of
faith in his ultimate recovery, which paves the way for what is to come. The
parallels between this tablet and Job are even more striking as can be seen
in the following examples:

Ludlul 2.4 – I called to my god, but he did not show his face.
Job 13.24 – Why do you hide your face, and count me as your enemy?
Job 34.29 – When he is quiet, who can condemn?
When he hides his face, who can behold him, whether it be a nation or an
   individual?

Ludlul 2.23 – For myself, I gave attention to supplication and prayer:
24 To me prayer was discretion, sacrifice my rule.
25 The day for reverencing the god was a joy to my heart.
Job 16.17 – There is no violence in my hands, and my prayer is pure.
Job 1.5 – He [Job] would rise early in the morning and offer burnt offerings according to the number of them all.

Ludlul 2. 36 – Who knows the will of the gods in heaven?
37 Who understands the plans of the underworld gods?
38 Where have mortals learnt the way of a god?
Job 28.23 – God understands the way to it [wisdom] and he knows its place.

Ludlul 2.50 – Debilitating Disease is let loose upon me.
Job 30.18 – With violence ['by the great force of my disease' in some translations]
   he seizes my garment; he grasps me by the collar of my tunic.

Ludlul 2.60 – My face is gloomy, my eyes are in flood.
Job 16.16 – My face is red with weeping, and deep darkness is on my eyelids.

Ludlul 2.63 – They affected my flesh and caused convulsions.
Job 7.5 – My flesh is clothed with worms and dirt;
my skin hardens, then breaks out again.
Job 19.20 – My bones cling to my skin and to my flesh,
and I have escaped by the skin of my teeth.

Ludlul 2.73 – My eyes stare, but do not see
74 My ears are open, but do not hear.
75 Feebleness has seized my whole body.
76 Concussion has fallen upon my flesh.
Job 21.6 – When I think of it I am dismayed, and shuddering seizes my flesh.
Job 14.22 – They feel only the pain of their own bodies [flesh] and mourn only for
   themselves.

Ludlul 2. 90 – My malady is indeed protracted.
91 Through lack of food my countenance is changed,
Job 6.7 My appetite refuses to touch them; they are like food that is loathsome
   to me.
Job 16.8 – He has shrivelled me up which is a witness against me;
My leanness has risen up against me, and it testifies to my face.

Ludlul 2. 92 – My flesh is flaccid, and my blood has ebbed away
93 My bones have come apart, and are covered (only) with my skin.
94 My tissues are inflamed, and have caught the...-disease.
Job 16.8 b – My leanness has risen up against me, and it testifies to my face.
Job 19.20 – 'My bones cling to my skin and to my flesh, and I have escaped by the
   skin of my teeth.'

Ludlul 2. 96 – My house has become my prison.
97 My arms are stricken – which shackles my flesh;
98 My feet are limp – which fetters my person.
99 My afflictions are grievous, my wound is severe.
Job 1.10a – Have you not put a fence around him and his house and all that he has,
   on every side?
Job 34.6b – My wound is incurable, though I am without transgression.
Job 36.8 – And if they are bound in fetters and caught in the cords of affliction...

Ludlul 2. 102 – All day long the tormentor torments [me]
103 Nor at night does he let me relax for a minute.

Job 7.4 – When I lie down I say, 'When shall I rise?' But the night is long, and I am
full of tossing until dawn.

Ludlul 2.106 – I spend the night in my dung like an ox,
107 And wallow in my excrement like a sheep.
Job 2.8 – Job took a potsherd with which to scrape himself, and sat among the ashes
[on the dungheap].
Job 7.5a – My flesh is clothed with worms and dirt.

Tablet 3 starts with the words, 'His hand was heavy upon me', presumably
describing Marduk's hand. There then follows a series of dreams or psychic
experiences in which different characters appear, the net effect of which is
that Marduk seems appeased. The restoration begins with disease demons
being taken away so that the evil illness can be countered. The ending is
fragmentary but it is clear that the sufferer goes through a river ordeal, has a
slave mark removed and then walks along the streets of Babylon to the temple of Marduk declaring that he is an example to all who have sinned against
Marduk. At this point it seems that the sufferer is owning his sin. Marduk
then suppresses all his human enemies and the text breaks off. There are
fewer correspondences here, although I have found some as follows:

Ludlul 3. 1 – His hand was heavy upon me, I could not bear it.
2 My dread of him was alarming, it…[me]
Job 13.21 – Withdraw your hand far from me, and do not let dread of you
terrify me.
Job 19.21 – Have pity on me, have pity on me, O you my friends,
for the hand of God has touched me!
Job 30.21 – You have turned cruel to me, with the might of your hand you
persecute me.
Job 33.7 – No fear of me need terrify you; my pressure will not be heavy on you.

Ludlul 3.7 – Day and night alike I groan,
8 In dream and waking moments I am equally wretched.
Job 7.4 – When I lie down I say' When shall I rise?' But the night is long, and I am
full of tossing until dawn.
Job 23.2 – Today also my complaint is bitter, his hand is heavy despite my groaning.

Tablet 4 narrates the saving of the sufferer by Marduk. Seeing his recovery,
the citizens of Babylon burst into acclamation of Marduk and his consort.
The sufferer passes through eleven gates of the Esagil temple complex in
Babylon and at each receives a blessing. Once inside, the speaker suppli-
cates to Marduk and offers him a feast. The sacrifice offered by Job on

behalf of the friends as a part of the happy ending in Job (42.8-9) is perhaps the only parallel here.

It is the second tablet that clearly bears most resemblance to Job, although there are also some significant parallels in the first. The whole text was nicknamed 'The Babylonian Job' largely on the basis of parallels of Job with the earlier tablets. The wider poem is arguably less close. The dream aspect that comes out in tablet 3 is interesting (cf. Eliphaz (4.12-17), Elihu (33.15) (see Johnson, 2009). It was David Clines (1994) who argued that the whole of Job was a bad dream by a rich person imagining he suddenly lost everything! It could be likened to mantic wisdom, a later branch of wisdom that emphasizes dreams, thought to have its origin in Sumero-Babylonian thought (see L.G. Perdue, 2008).

b. *THE BABYLONIAN* THEODICY

This second major work from Babylon is a Dialogue between a sufferer and one friend in the form of an acrostic poem. The sufferer is concerned with social injustice. The friend, like Job's friends, maintains the traditional view that piety leads to prosperity and that the divine ordering of the universe is just. Issues such as why human beings oppress one another are raised and the idea that a personal god can provide protection is rejected. The sufferer and his friend agree that the gods made human beings prone to injustice. The friend airs the idea of human limitation in the understanding of sin and the remoteness of the gods who alone can reveal a person's sin. There is also a note of resignation in the suggestion by the sufferer that he might give up all social responsibilities and live the life of a vagrant. His friend rebukes him for such a thought, appealing to the sacredness of institutions that he would be leaving behind. Overall, however, the debate remains polite throughout.

In what follows I will go through the main themes of each of the twenty-seven sections that make up the text. The resonances with Job will be obvious by now.

In section one (I) we learn the sufferer's tale of woe. He was born late to his parents who died and left him an orphan. He asks, Why do the gods (notably 'his goddess' in this context) not protect those who cannot protect themselves? Why do the powerful oppress such? Why has the first-born advantages over the later child? The friend replies in section two (II) that the sufferer is being unnecessarily despondent and that the death of parents is part of the common lot of humankind. The hard life of the sufferer is acknowledged and put in the context of the nexus between prosperity and piety. The description of the sufferer's demeanour recalls Job's 'eyes…dim with grief' motif:

II.15 You have reduced your beaming face to scowls.

II. 22 The humble man who fears his goddess accumulates wealth.

The sufferer responds in section three (III) that his desperate state has not been appreciated – he knows no way out. Similar sentiments to Job abound in this section such as his call to be heard and his description of his physical suffering.

III.25-6 I will ask you a question; listen to what I say.

Pay attention for a moment hear my words

III. 27-30 My body is a wreck, emaciation darkens [me]

My success has vanished, my stability has gone.

My strength is enfeebled, my prosperity has ended,

Moaning and grief have blackened my features.

The friend replies in section four (IV) that a life of piety does not go unrewarded.

IV.42-4 Ever seek the [correct standards] of justice.

Your…, the mighty one, will show kindness,

[…] will grant mercy.

In section five (V) the sufferer cites examples of crimes which pay – animal and human examples are used. This recalls Job's citation of situations in which the wicked appear to prosper as in chap. 21. The polite language used by the sufferer to the friend echoes that of the three friends of Job – Job himself is less concerned about offending them! Recalling past religious observance has a parallel in Job's scrupulous behaviour as described in 1.5.

V. 45 I bow to you, my comrade, I grasp your wisdom.

V. 54-5 [Have I] held back offerings? I have prayed to my god,

[I have] pronounced the blessing over the goddess's regular sacrifices…

In section six (VI) the friend cites traditional teaching about the remoteness and inscrutability of the divine mind which compares to Job's complaint about God's distance (e.g. 11.7-9) and links up with the God speeches too. In addition, criminals meet a dire end and the sufferer must not be tempted into crime. Rather, the sufferer needs to cultivate the gods.

VI. 58-9 You are as stable as the earth, but the plan of the gods is remote.

Look at the superb wild ass on the [plain;]

VI. 65-6 Do you wish to go the way these have gone?

Rather seek the lasting reward of (your) god!

This explanation does not satisfy the sufferer who describes in section seven (VII) how his life of dedication to religion has only resulted in his present state and he accuses his friend of blasphemy.

VII 72-3 In my youth I sought the will of my god;

With prostration and prayer I followed my goddess.

VII.77 The rogue has been promoted, but I have been brought low.

VII. 79-80 You have forsaken right and blaspheme against your god's designs.

In your mind you have an urge to disregard the divine ordinances.

The friend sees this accusation as blasphemy but remains polite and reiterates in section eight (VIII) that it is a hard thing to grasp the wisdom of the gods.

VIII.78-9 My reliable fellow, holder of knowledge, your thoughts are perverse.

You have forsaken right and blaspheme against your god's designs.

VIII.82 The plans of the god [...] like the centre of heaven.

After a gap, the friend points out the joys of a life of simple piety, of performing duties to society and the gods (XII).

XII.127 [I] cared for...[I] looked after the young [ones...].

The sufferer retorts that all he desires is to escape from society and live as a vagrant (XIII). This is not a path that Job goes down.

XIII.133-4 I will abandon my home...

I will desire no property...

The next three sections are rather fragmentary, but these passages strike a chord with Job – the rebuke of the friend in XIV, the response from the sufferer in XV that nothing is stable or guaranteed and the response from the friend in XVI calling for humility in the face of the gods.

XIV. 147 Your reason has left you...

XV. 164-5 Should I seek a son and daughter [...]

May I not lose what I find...

XVI.166 Humble and submissive one...

The full text resumes in seventeen (XVII) with the sufferer emphasizing how easily rich and poor change positions.

XVII.187 The owner of wealth is fallen. [His...] is far away.

Sections eighteen (XVIII) and nineteen (XIX) are fragmentary whilst twenty is fuller (XX). In XX the friend is saying that piety does pay. The rebuke to the sufferer is a bit stronger.

XX.212-13 You have let your subtle mind go astray.
…you have ousted wisdom.
XX. 219-20 Follow in the way of the god, observe his rites,
…is counted as righteousness.

The sufferer replies in the fragmentary section twenty-one (XXI) that the unscrupulous are those who become wealthy (cf. Job's complaints about the prosperity of the wicked, e.g. chap. 21).

XXI. 223 – They amass goods…

The friend repeats in twenty-two (XXII) that in the end the wicked are discomfited but the god-fearing never starve, although they may not have an abundance.

XXII. 239-40 Unless you seek the will of the god, what luck have you?
He that bears his god's yoke never lacks food, though it be sparse.

The sufferer then in section twenty-three (XXIII) contrasts the privileges and arrogance of the first-born as compared with others. His abject state is the outcome of his piety.

XXIII. 251-3 How have I profited that I have bowed down to my god?
I have to bow beneath the base fellow that meets me;
The dregs of humanity, like the rich and opulent, treat me with contempt.

In section twenty-four (XXIV) the friend replies that the first-born is physically inferior to later offspring (apparently when women had children very young this could happen) and so the first-born privileges are offset. The ways of the divine cannot be fully known (cf. the tone of the God speeches in Job).

XXIV 256-7 The divine mind, like the centre of the heavens, is remote;
Knowledge of it is difficult; the masses do not know it.

The sufferer now says in section twenty-five (XXV) that the rich and powerful get away with false witness against the poor, and thus grind them down a theme reminiscent of Job's complaints in Job 20, 24 and 34.

XXV.271-4 They fill the [store-house] of the oppressor with gold,
But empty the larder of the beggar of its provisions.
They support the powerful, whose…is guilt,
But destroy the weak and drive away the powerless.

The friend agrees in section twenty-six that lies and false witness are part of human nature as the gods made it.

XXVI.279-80 [The gods] gave perverse speech to the human race.

With lies, and not truth, they endowed them for ever.
XXVI. 285-6 Making him [the poor man] suffer every evil like a crimi-
nal, because he has no protection.
Terrifyingly they bring him to his end, and extinguish him like a flame.

Having won his point, the sufferer concludes the Dialogue in section twenty-
seven (XXVII) with a plea that his friend contemplate his grief and that the
gods resume their protection, for he hasn't as yet received any assurances.
XXVII.289-90 I, though humble, wise, and a suppliant,
Have not seen help and succour for one moment.

Spending time with these texts helps to appreciate the close similarities with
the book of Job and adds fuel to the idea of a common currency of texts not
just of lament but also of questioning the justice of the gods that were preva-
lent in the Babylonian world in particular. These texts may well have influenced the Job author in some way – especially if he came into contact with
them in the wake of the Babylonian exile – but such questions of influence are
hard to know. The influence is mainly thematic rather than there being exact
intertextual parallels. However, the influence is undoubtedly there and gives
us a broader picture of Job's themes within their wider cultural context.

3. The Friends' Speeches in the Dialogue

In most of the ancient Near Eastern examples part of the suffering for the sufferer is his rejection by family and friends. In the Babylonian theodicy there is
one friend who acts as a sounding board for the sufferer. In Job, by contrast,
four friends act in this sounding board role and it is opportune to look at these
speeches with the ancient Near Eastern sentiments fresh in our minds. The
book of Job is perhaps unique in containing such a long Dialogue with friends,
used by the author as a vehicle of airing different sides of the issues, rather
than simply presenting the view of the lamenter himself. In what follows I will
outline the main arguments of the friends in the various rounds of speeches.
The friends are often characterized as saying exactly the same things as each
other, but arguably they do each have distinctive contributions to make. I
shall include the speeches of Elihu, the fourth, younger friend who is not
announced in the prologue, and whose speeches may be a later addition.
However, in the book as it stands, his is an important further contribution.

a. Round One

Eliphaz opens the debate in chap. 4. He begins tentatively – he doesn't want
to offend Job but he cannot restrain his words. This is in ironic contrast to

the silence in which the friends sat with Job, as described in 2.13. Eliphaz reminds Job of the support that he gave to others in the past with his own comforting words and then accuses him of impatience when he is the one suffering. Where now is his fear of God (cf. 1.1)? Eliphaz then launches into the line that all the friends will take, the fact that the upright are rewarded and the wicked are punished. One interesting aspect of this speech of Eliphaz is his description from verse 12 of a night vision in which a 'form' speaks to ask whether mortals can indeed be righteous before God. The inference is that human beings are nothing in the face of the godhead – they are easily crushed and destroyed. They are not pure and innocent, indeed the human condition is to be sinful. The use of an appeal to a dream is unusual in mainstream wisdom and has closer connections to mantic wisdom (Perdue, 2008) or even apocalyptic (Johnson, 2010).

In chap. 5 Eliphaz asks Job if he has any divine support. He goes on to a description of the fool, continuing his argument that humans tend towards 'trouble' (verse 7). He then takes on a rather pious tone in his advocacy of the true path, i.e. trusting in God. He praises God's wondrous works, his support of the poor and lowly and his corresponding punishment of the schemer. He encourages Job not to react against God's disciplinary punishment, for it will only be a temporary chastisement, designed to put him back on track after his misdeeds have been punished. He sees God as ultimately wishing to redeem and protect his servants. He therefore affirms all the good things that will come to the righteous – safety, many descendants, a long life. These are just around the corner for Job if he has the right attitude towards his suffering.

The second friend, Bildad, speaks in his turn after Job has responded to Eliphaz. He accuses Job directly of 'windy words'. He very much maintains the traditional line that God's punishment is just. Job's children must have sinned against God. It is just a matter of seeking God and of good behaviour. He muses for a few verses on the transience of life, but believes in an accumulated wisdom that comes down to human beings and which he is now citing. He goes on from verse 11 to describe the fate of the godless. Any seeming prosperity is temporary and their presence is quickly forgotten. Bildad uses rich imagery here of plants and spiders. Such use of imagery by the author is a keynote of the book. Like Eliphaz Bildad sees a brighter future for Job if only he will acknowledge his guilt and move on. He firmly believes that God is on the side of the blameless and innocent person.

Zophar, the third friend, now takes his turn. He also sees Job as full of talk and babble. He expresses the view that God would soon put Job right in his claim to have done nothing wrong were God to appear and speak to Job. This is an ironic anticipation of the God-speeches, where God doesn't directly counter Job's claim of innocence and hence does not directly vindicate Zophar's position. Zophar takes the line that Job cannot know the greatness of God, nor hope to contain God, nor can Job change the judgements on people that God makes. Zophar tries to make Job feel both small and stupid (v. 12). The proverb he cites here suggests that a stupid person will never get understanding just as a wild ass cannot be born human. So too Job will never understand what God does. Zophar then exhorts Job to reconsider his attitude, put away iniquity and come back to God. He paints a picture of a rosy future and ends on a note of punishment of the wicked.

b. *Round Two*

Eliphaz in chap. 15 continues the 'words/speaking' theme that runs through the book and accuses Job, indirectly, of verbosity – ironic since that is exactly what the friends are guilty of too! A Dialogue form rather encourages verbosity by its very nature! He accuses Job of not fearing God in all this talking – too many words hinder quiet mediation and his words alone prove his guilt. He sees Job as rather arrogant in his defiance over his innocence, and as having an over-inflated view of his own ego. When he asks Job in verse 7 if he is the firstborn of the human race, it is a rhetorical question expecting the answer 'of course not'! It is perhaps Wisdom that he is referring to here, who in Proverbs 8 is alongside God in the formation of the world. Does Job claim to have all wisdom on a par with God? This is his arrogance, to think that he knows all the answers. What does Job know that the friends don't? They are all older men and wisdom is seen to reside with the old. He is concerned about Job's defiant attitude. He backs up Zophar's view that human beings cannot be wholly pure in verse 14 and so God comes down hard on sinners. Eliphaz claims to know wisdom inherited from his forebears. He knows about the punishment of the wicked. In this description of the wicked from verse 20 Eliphaz tries to frighten Job stressing their pain, despair, hunger and so on. Any fleeting prosperity such as riches will not endure and emptiness will be the keynotes of their lives. Again rich imagery of grapes and blossoms is used, as well as more adversarial battle imagery.

Bildad speaks in chap. 18 and again begins with the words and speaking theme. He is tired of Job treating the friends as stupid and he tries, like Eliphaz, to bring Job down a peg or two. He affirms the fate of the wicked – their light that will become dark. He uses the imagery of steps, paths and nets which is characteristic of wisdom in Proverbs. The wicked fall into traps, they are frightened by terrors all around them (imagined or real) and they are hungry and often ill. Although the friends speak in general terms about the wicked, there often is the inference that Job is really the target of their descriptions. The worst fate of the wicked is the lack of remembrance of them and then their lack of descendants. Again Bildad tries to frighten Job with his description – such a fate is surely not one that Job would want!

Finally Zophar has his turn in chap. 20. He sees Job wandering off the point in his diatribe and so asks him to pay attention. He is agitated on Job's behalf, insulted by Job's attitude and inspired by what he calls 'a spirit beyond my understanding', presumably God himself. He then again reiterates the fate of the wicked – their prosperity is shortlived, fleeting and insubstantial; their lives will be short, their children will be brought low and they too will live short lives. The veneer of 'sweetness' that they give off, is just that, a veneer, and, continuing the food imagery, it is like poison in their stomachs. They can't keep prosperity down for long, just as someone who is about to be sick cannot keep food down. Thus their misdeeds will rebound on them and none of their efforts will be lasting. This food and eating imagery continues for some verses. They ate everything up, thus leaving nothing to be eaten in the future – thus they robbed themselves of their own future. Instead God's wrath will fill their bellies. Warlike imagery follows in verse 24 – the wicked will be struck through with an arrow which will pierce their bodies and they will lose their health as well as their livelihood. Again, this is a galling description, designed to frighten Job.

c. *Round Three*

Round three is the incomplete round in which Bildad's speech is short and Zophar's non-existent. I have already discussed verses that could be ascribed to each of them in the discussion of Job's speeches and so will not revisit those. In this round then we have a speech of Eliphaz and one from Bildad. There is a sense of the arguments of the friends tailing off, largely because of their repetitious quality, whilst Job himself gains ground – perhaps this is therefore a deliberate technique by the author.

Eliphaz resumes in chap. 22. He puts his question slightly differently in his wondering of what use human beings can be to God. The inference is that their use is minimal to God, whether wise or wicked, anyway and so even less use when wickedness abounds. This is an indirect way of broaching his usual point that Job must have sinned since God does not punish piety. God makes a direct accusation of Job regarding good deeds that he has failed to do (vv. 6-7) – he has exacted false pledges from his family, stripped the naked of clothes (i.e. taken clothing off poor people), neglected to help out the weary with basic drink and withheld bread from the hungry. This is because, as one of the powerful, he ignored those lower down on the social scale. He is also accused of not helping out widows and orphans. This accusation directly counters Job's claim to have done all he could for the poor, lowly and oppressed. Eliphaz wants to make it clear that Job's suffering is directly deserved. From verse 12 he restates God's might and wisdom. He sees Job as belittling God's greatness, following in the paths of the wicked of old. He also restates the traditional doctrine of the punishment of the wicked despite a temporary respite. Eliphaz calls Job back to God and to a good relationship with him. He paints a rosy picture of restoration, mentioning gold and silver and all good things. Like the descriptions of the wicked, the picture of the righteous is also overdone – rhetoric is the art of persuasion here.

The final speech of Bildad in chap. 25 as it stands is very short. He begins by stating God's supremacy. The peace that reigns in heaven contrasts with the armies that God can set upon the wicked. God is so great that human beings pale in comparison and the point is made again about the sinfulness of humankind. Humans are compared to maggots and worms, they are so small in the sight of God. Zophar's third speech is missing unless we reconstruct it from the speeches of Job, as suggested in chap. 3.

4. *The Elihu Speeches*

The final word is left to Elihu, a young fourth friend who appears seemingly from nowhere, but claims to have been listening to the entire debate. In some ways he functions like a chorus in a Greek tragedy – he is the onlooker, the outsider who nevertheless wants his chance to speak. Elihu is not introduced at any stage and is the youngster who didn't like to speak out whilst the more senior friends were speaking. Since he both repeats former material and anticipates later (although he also has points of his own to make) there is a sense of superfluity about his speeches. This has led scholars to evaluate them very differently – everything from their being the key to the book to their being repetitive and tiresome and an unnecessary addition. He is described as the son of Barachel the Buzite of the family of Ram (32.2, 6) – this is a good Israelite family with Davidic connections. Interestingly he is not from an extra-Israelite context (notably Edomite) as the other friends appear to be.

At the beginning of chaps. 32-7, that contain these speeches, we are told that the three friends replied to Job no longer. This is the point at which Elihu decides to speak, out of anger. Speaking out angrily is not usually recommended by the wise so this is a surprising emphasis. Elihu is angry at Job's self-justification at God's expense and he is angry at the friends for not having provided satisfactory answers. Because of his youth, Elihu had hesitated to speak, but now he decides to have his turn. The first five verses of this chapter are prose, then we move into the speech itself. Although wisdom is said to be with the aged, Elihu disputes that point and claims that the divine spirit itself leads a person to real understanding. He explains his reticence and his criticism of the friends' replies – he will now speak out: in fact he is bursting to speak!

Elihu starts his speech in chap. 33 by referring to words, mouth, tongue – the language of communication. He addresses Job, claims divine inspiration, and then cites Job's position. He tells Job that he is not right to claim innocence and then call God his enemy. He states God's greatness and otherness. God can speak in different ways to people, through dreams to deter them from evil deeds or through suffering. A person can be on the verge of death, but if that person's mediator then proclaims the sufferer upright, deliverance is nigh. God can even restore the sinner without payback. God can bring people back from the brink of death. All this is true in abstract terms, but is addressed to Job in particular.

At the beginning of chap. 34 Elihu addresses the friends once more. He also cites Job and accuses him of aligning himself with the wicked. God is always in the right – people are judged according to their deeds. It is wrong to criticize God who in his greatness created the world and could uncreate it just as easily. Elihu sees it as an impossibility that the ruler of the world could hate justice. God judges justly and shows no partiality to rich or poor – they all suffer the same fate, which is death. God is all-seeing and all-knowing and there is no hiding from his presence. God can bring the mighty down or raise others up, but it is always according to justice since God knows all human secrets and deeds. If God chooses to remain hidden too, no individual or nation is in a position to judge this behaviour. Elihu reiterates at the end of his speech that God does not pay people back (i.e. Job) according to what they think they have deserved, rather it is how God evaluates their behaviour that matters.

In the next chapter Elihu condemns self-righteous behaviour such as Job shows. He asks Job a series of questions – what does he gain from maintaining his innocence? If Job has indeed sinned, as Elihu believes he has, then he is simply adding to his sin by doing so. Nor does Job show concern for the way his actions affect others. Suffering is common, as is calling out to God, but God does not answer those who show pride (itself a manifestation of wickedness) or non-recognition of God. Hence Job cannot force God to answer and so, in Elihu's view, he is wasting his words.

In chap. 36 Elihu's words continue – he too could be accused of verbosity! He claims to speak what is true on God's behalf. He emphasizes God's might and understanding, and maintains that God kills off the wicked and promotes the cause of the oppressed. Those who are righteous prosper, but if they overreach themselves in arrogance that is punished. If they listen to God and then they can still expect lives of prosperity. But for those who do not listen there is nothing but death, usually premature. He accuses Job of obsession with his case (i.e. that of the wicked) and warns that his arguing is in danger of turning him further away from God. He tells Job not to turn to iniquity in attempting to tell God what to do or accuse God of wrongdoing. God is great and unknowable and human beings are wrong to judge God. God is the creator and he governs society too. God is angry when wickedness abounds.

Finally in chap. 37 Elihu rounds off his speech. He expresses his awe at God's majesty here, his heart trembling at God's voice of thunder. He extols God's might in creation from snow and rain to ice and winds. Natural elements are at his command. He anticipates what God has to say by asking Job what he knows of the workings of creation in a series of rhetorical questions. Of course Job can't spread out the skies as God does! Humans cannot argue with such a powerful one as God. God's majesty is such that all human beings should do is fear him. God's essence is justice and those who are not wise will be rightly punished.

Elihu puts a similar stress as the friends did on Job's self-righteousness and on his need to accept that he has sinned. He emphasizes, even more than they, the nature of God and God's promoting of justice. He claims to have insight into the divine realm and uses that as his point of authority in preaching to Job. He starts to anticipate the God speeches in his expression of God's otherness, might and power in creation.

We saw above how Dialogue is an important medium for the conveying of ideas in the Babylonian Theodicy in particular. This is clearly the case in Job where traditional viewpoints are reflected in the friends' speeches, although I have tried to show that they do not speak with one voice (as the single friend inevitably does in the Theodicy) but with nuance and variation. Elihu in particular has his own stance and emphasis. Although the friends of Job are often portrayed as less than helpful to him, the Theodicy parallel shows how sometimes such friends help to keep the sufferer (whose complaint may well have overcome his more moderate reasoning) to keep a sense of balance. When the sufferer in the Theodicy thinks that he might give up his social responsibilities and become a vagrant, he is quickly rebuked by the friend. Job too has vast mood-swings and the friends in their own way are trying to keep him focused on what he, like them, had believed to be the case before his calamities fell upon him.

Bibliography

Works cited

G. von Rad 'Job 38 and Ancient Egyptian Wisdom', in *The Problem of the Hexateuch and Other Essays* (Edinburgh & London: Oliver & Boyd, 1966), pp. 281-291.

J. Day, 'Foreign Semitic Influence on the Wisdom of Israel and Its appropriation in the Book of Proverbs', in *Wisdom in Ancient Israel: Essays in honour of J.A. Emerton* (Cambridge, Cambridge University Press, 1995), pp. 55-70.

S.N. Kramer, *History begins at Sumer* (London: Thames and Hudson, 1958).

W.G. Lambert, *Babylonian Wisdom Literature* (Oxford: Oxford University Press, 1960).

J. Gray, 'The Book of Job in the Context of Near Eastern Literature', *ZAW*, 82 (1970), pp. 251-269.

T.J. Johnson, *Now my Eye Sees You: Unveiling an Apocalyptic Job* (Sheffield: Sheffield Phoenix Press, 2009).

D.J.A. Clines, 'Why is There are Book of Job and What Does It Do to You if You Read It?' in *The Book of Job*, ed W A M Beuken, Bibliotheca ephemeridum theologicarum lovaniensium 114 (Leuven: Louvain University Press, 1994), pp. 1-20.

L.G. Perdue, *The Sword and the Stylus: An Introduction to Wisdom in the Age of Empires* (Grand Rapids MI: W B Eerdmans, 2008) Chapter 8.

Main Texts

'I will praise the Lord of Wisdom' in J.B. Pritchard, *Ancient Near Eastern Texts relating to the Old Testament* (Princeton, NJ: Princeton University Press, 3rd edn, 1969.) 434. Also called 'The poem of the righteous sufferer' in W.H. Hallo & K. Lawson Younger Jr, *The Context of Scripture* Leiden: Brill, 1997, 486-492 and found in a new version by Annus Amar and Alan Lenzi, *Ludlul Bel Nemeqi: the Standard Poem of the Righteous Sufferer*. State Archives of Assyria Cuneiform Texts 7 (Helsinki: The New-Assyrian Corpus Project, 2010).

'The Babylonian Theodicy' in W.G. Lambert, *Babylonian Wisdom Literature* (1960: 63-91) or in J.B. Pritchard, *Ancient Near Eastern Texts* (1969: 438-440) or in *The Context of Scripture*, 1997, pp. 492-495.

S.N. Kramer, 'Man and his God': A Sumerian Variation on the 'Job' motif' in *Wisdom in Israel and in the ANE*, ed. M. Noth and D.W. Thomas, VTS, 3 (1955), pp. 170-182. Also in *The Context of Scripture*, 1997, pp. 573-575.

Further Reading

M. Jastrow, 'A Babylonian Parallel to the Story of Job,' *JBL*, 25 (1906), pp. 135-191.

J.L. Crenshaw, *Old Testament Wisdom: An Introduction* (Louisville KY: Westminster John Knox Press, 2010, 3rd edn) Chapter 9.

K.J. Dell, *Get Wisdom, Get Insight: An Introduction to Israel's wisdom literature* (London: DLT, 2000) Chapter 7.

R. Gordis, *The Book of God and Man* (Chicago: University of Chicago Press, 1965), Chapter 5.

R.G. Albertson, 'Job and Ancient Near Eastern Wisdom Literature', *Scripture in Context II: More Essays on the Comparative Method* (ed. W. Hallo, J. Moyer and L.G. Perdue Winona Lake, IN: Eisenbrauns, 1983), pp. 213-230.

M. Weinfeld, 'Job and its Mesopotamian Parallels – a typological analysis', *Text and Context: Old Testament and Semitic Studies for F C Fensham*, JSOTS, 48 (ed. W. Claasen, Sheffield: JSOT, 1988), pp. 217-226.

5

THEOLOGICAL ISSUES RAISED BY THE BOOK OF JOB

It is in the realm of theology that Job makes its greatest impact. There are three major themes in Job which intersect and overlap. The first, based primarily on the emphasis of the Prologue and Epilogue is the theme of disinterested righteousness. 'Does Job fear God for nothing?' (1.9) as the Satan asks. What is Job's motivation for his faith – is it genuinely his fear of God or is it for reasons of personal prosperity and wealth? The second is the problem of retributive justice as aired in the Dialogue between Job and the friends. Is suffering always the result of punishment for some misdeeds or can there ever be cases where the maxim of reward for the pious and judgement for the wicked does not work? In the case of a truly innocent sufferer such as Job, how is retributive justice to be understood and can it be maintained? Job's own protest against the traditional arguments of the friends opens up issues of how human beings react to suffering of a severe kind. The third and arguably most theological of the three themes is the relationship between God and humanity as seen primarily in the God speeches and Job's responses. This is essentially the question, how can one be in a relationship with God that is meaningful when one feels that one has been mistreated by God? This links up with the problem of misplaced retributive justice, but it goes beyond that to question whether human beings can have (or would want) a relationship with a God who, it seems, can behave in capricious or unexpected ways. Issues such as the nature of God and of God's justice (the problem of theodicy) and the purpose of human existence are implicit in this debate. In what follows I shall look at these three main scholarly evaluations of the Job theme and air the theological issues raised by emphasis on them. I shall also air the suggestion that Job may be likened to tragedy as a useful means for drawing out the radical nature of the book's theological message. Finally I shall consider the God speeches as my key text, arguably the theological 'nub' of the whole book.

1. Disinterested Righteousness

If one simply reads Job as a 'story', putting emphasis on the narrative parts of the book, as many early interpreters did, then it is natural enough to see the crux of the debate as being the issue of Job's righteousness as aired in the prose sections of the book. Job is held up by God in his interaction with the Satan as a model of righteous behaviour, such that God uses him as his prime example in the heavenly discussion. Indeed the first thing we are told about Job is that he is 'blameless and upright' (1.1) and it is on this presupposition that the book stands. It is the Satan who puts the note of doubt into the debate when he questions the motivation for Job's righteousness – is he simply being righteous because of all the material rewards that he has enjoyed? Or is his righteousness truly altruistic? God's choice of Job would suggest that God believes Job's righteousness to be altruistic, but God agrees to the Satan's testing in order to prove the point further. Job's reactions in the prologue are much as one would expect from a pious person – he abases himself in mourning at the loss of children and property (1.20) but God says 'Naked I came from my mother's womb, and naked shall I return there: the LORD gave and the LORD has taken away; blessed be the name of the LORD.' (1.21) He goes on praising God despite the apparent injustice, and indeed he does not acknowledge God's behaviour as unjust, seeing God as having the right to bless or withdraw his blessing at will. Y. Hoffman writes of Job's reaction in the Prologue that it 'clearly illuminates his view that God owes him nothing and does not even need to justify his deeds, since he only took away what he had previously voluntarily given.' (Hoffman, 1981: 163) In this reaction Job, even in the Prologue, is going against traditional wisdom ideas that the righteous should be rewarded and the wicked punished, as aired in the Dialogue. It is stressed in the text that even when tested in this way 'Job did not sin or charge God with wrongdoing.' (1.22) This is the main focus of the narration of this prose story – that Job continued to fear God and to behave in a righteous manner. After the second test of the inflicting of a terrible disease Job maintains his position 'Shall we receive the good at the hand of God, and not receive the bad?' (2.10) and again it is reiterated by the narrator 'in all this Job did not sin with his lips'.

If we then jump to the Epilogue we find Job vindicated in what he has said by God – 'the LORD said to Eliphaz the Temanite: 'My wrath is kindled against you and against your two friends: for you have not spoken of me what is right, as my servant Job has.' (42.7) In a purely prose context one could read this statement as referring to the pious words of Job in the Prologue and the corresponding silence of the friends in the Prologue, as some commentators have done. However, it is more normally seen as a comment referring to the whole Dialogue and hence confirming Job's right to speak out. Job then performs a sacrifice on behalf of the friends and his prayer is accepted (42.8-9). Then Job's fortunes are restored with a new set of children and all seems to be happy. So the moral of the prose tale is that Job's piety was indeed disinterested and if one holds on to faith in God, even in a situation of darkest adversity, it will come out all right in the end. Or will it?

Somehow this conclusion sounds a bit trite in the light of actual human experience. If we scratch under the surface of the story it is not hard to find a few anomalies on both ethical and theological grounds. Let us start with the character of God. The first point is that God even allows Job to be tested by the Satan – what kind of God submits the most loyal servants to such a test? We know of other such tests from the Old Testament, such as that of Abraham in Genesis 22, so one could argue that this was along similar lines. However, God's motivation for doing so is open to question. Carl Jung (1979) argued that God felt threatened by the Satan at this point and allows himself to be influenced by a 'doubting thought'. Whybray found any number of reasons possible – to gain more information about Job's real character, to salvage his own dignity or even for idle entertainment. He concludes 'In any case the picture presented of God in these chapters is hardly a flattering one.' (Whybray 2000: 15) Then there is the very fact of a wager at Job's expense – he is after all the one who suffers simply in the interest of proving a divine point. It may be worthwhile in theological terms to contemplate testing God's virtue, but the devastating consequence for the individual and his friends and family might make one question its validity. As Oesterley and Robinson ask, 'Is God justified in torturing a perfectly good and innocent person, merely to prove that he is good and innocent?' (1934: 176).

Then there is the Satan who actually does the inflicting – perhaps this is what we are to learn to expect of this character, who as yet is unknown to us within the pages of the Old Testament. The Satan's role is first to place the doubt in the mind of God (cf. the serpent placing doubt in Eve's mind about the tree of knowledge in the garden of Eden in Gen 3.4-5) and then to carry out the task. His question 'Does Job fear God for nothing?' (1.9) is an accusation to God of protectionism to such an extent that Job has a vested interest in behaving righteously. With this question the Satan arguably instigates the whole situation to which God must respond. So maybe the blame should rather attach to him. His actual inflicting of the calamities also seems to exonerate God and to distance him from the testing itself. God hands power over to Satan in 1.12 and 2.6. However, this handover is only temporary and does not threaten God's ultimate control over the situation and so in that sense he is still in charge. It is interesting that throughout the Dialogue both Job and the friends assume that it is God who has done the inflicting and not the Satan and that the Satan does not reappear in the Epilogue to do any blessing. We have also noted Job's reaction in which he seems not to expect any principle of justice to be working – he is just simply accepting of the gifts God either chooses to give or to take away. This might be seen as a licence to arbitrariness for God, for if there is no system of justice God can behave just as God likes, and what kind of God have we uncovered here?

2. *Retributive Suffering*

It seems with the Dialogue section that we are back on track in relation
to retributive justice. The sense that it is the dominating issue of the book
comes largely from the sheer number of chapters spent on the issue with
the Dialogue going back and forth between the friends and Job. The wisdom tradition as represented in Proverbs is clearly in the background of the
thought here, with its simple maxim that the good are rewarded and the
wicked punished. This is the view maintained by all four friends, including
the young Elihu, although, as we have seen, with various different nuances.
The authority that the accumulated knowledge of the wise has given to
the friends is a point of reference for them. There has to be a reason for
suffering and that must be, in this case, that Job has sinned (4.7). Indeed
they think him arrogant for denying this clear culpability – Zophar says in
barbed tone in 11.6, 'Know then that God exacts less of you than your guilt
deserves.' One answer to the conundrum is that this is a temporary chasten-
ing by God that will ultimately pass (5.17) and what Job needs to do is be
more accepting of this situation. Instead they see him as rude and obstinate
(8.2-3). They extol God's greatness and make the point that his justice is
greater than that of humans (e.g. 22.3) – a point with which Job would
agree, but in a more negative tone to the point of seeing God's actions as
beyond human attempts to rationalize them. This relates to God's ultimate
knowledge and wisdom which they all assume. Zophar says in chap. 11 that
he wishes God would tell Job 'the secrets of wisdom, for wisdom is many-
sided' (v. 6). God is seen here to hold the key to all wisdom, even that outside human understanding. Eliphaz too rebukes Job for thinking he knows
all the answers – 'Do you limit wisdom to yourself, What do you know that
we do not know? What do you understand that is not clear to us?' (15.8-9)
The issue of who holds knowledge is at stake here. The friends have the wisdom tradition to fall back on – does Job really think he knows better than
God? Elihu too attributes all human understanding to God and accuses Job
of speaking 'without knowledge' (34.35). This theme of human efforts to
know wisdom and God's ultimate grasp of it is taken up by God himself in
the God speeches and is, in my view, an important key for unlocking the
message of the book.

Job is the one, in this context, who rails against the principle of retributive justice. Whereas in the Prologue he had seemed accepting of no real
principle of justice in his acceptance of God's treatment of him, it is almost
like a different character who breaks in at chap. 3 bewailing his lot. In many
ways he becomes a more real character at this point, representative of suffering humanity who, in the face of misfortune, would be likely to rail against
God. We have seen how he parodies traditional sentiments to get across

the point that God has turned against him so that all he formerly assumed is open to question. God has hedged him in, rather than offering him beneficial protection; God has worn him out, rather than offering him succour; God is his enemy rather than his friend. It is clear that the object of his attack is ultimately God, although he has a few sarcastic words to say to the friends along the way. He feels that God has treated him unfairly – he expected more. As M Weiss writes, '[Job] refuses to accept what he sees and he cannot accept what his friends say. He therefore searches and beseeches God, demanding to be shown the whole truth, the world's eternal truth. In order to settle the controversy on earth, God will appear to Job and will show him the world in all its stark reality.' (Weiss 1983.82) His language starts to take on a legal tone as he speaks in terms of justice, a fair trial, God as accused but also judge, and the need for a mediator. He is trying to force God into the dock, trying to make this principle of justice one which God should answer in a court of law. He cries out 'Know then that God has put me in the wrong, and closed his net around me' (19.6). He feels that God is not listening – 'I cry to you and you do not answer me, I stand, and you merely look at me. You have turned cruel to me, with the might of your hand you persecute me.' (30.20-21) He comes to the conclusion (as, ironically, he did at the end of the Prologue) that God does not promote strict retributive justice – the wicked are often rewarded and the good are punished (30.26). But he lacks his former accepting attitude – rather this is the world turned upside-down. Job repeatedly asks God what sin he might have committed (13.23) but receives no answer. He asks for pardon (7.23), but then how can this be given to a non-existent sin? He longs for death (6.20), but then wonders if that is such a good idea after all given that he would not then be able to continue his argument with God. Job's lack of answers leads him to accuse God of cruelty – as Tsevat writes, 'In ever-repeated and diverse ways Job accuses God of wanton cruelty.' (Tsevat 1976: 345) It is only after God has spoken that Tsevat believes that Job reaches a higher level of understanding, although whether he receives a satisfactory answer or not is a moot point.

This theme has given many a teacher or preacher a way into talking about innocent suffering and how to comprehend it. There is a general feeling that life should be fair, if not all the time then some of it, and we find ourselves railing against God if it is not. In that context the words of Job have a fresh resonance, whether our response be more accepting as the Job of the prologue was, or more protesting as in the Dialogue. We may think that the friends have good arguments too. The question of the justice of God in his dealings in the lives of both individuals and communities has rung down the centuries. The ultimate question is Why me? Or even Why anyone? Why does anyone suffer and why do some appear to suffer more than others? This is Job's question too – why should one as God-fearing as he have had to cope with the loss of his children, his livelihood, his self-respect and his physical health? Isn't this too much for one person to bear?

3. *The God/Human Relationship*

It becomes clear as the Dialogue comes to a close and it ends with Job's final lament that it is God who needs to appear to justify himself. In modern scholarship the main theme of Job has generally been seen to be the relationship between God and human beings, especially as aired in the God speeches and in Job's responses and laments (Lacoque, 1996). C.A. Newsom (2003) stresses the importance of this God/human relationship theme in the Dialogue section as well as in the later sections of the book, whilst D.J. Pleins (1994) places an emphasis on the important part played by God's silence, a silence which allows Job time to grieve and to rise above the ensnared rationalizations of suffering offered by his friends. Y. Hoffman (1996) considers Job a 'blemished perfection', centrally concerned with the problem of God's justice, linking up with the theodicy issue.

Again, if we scratch under the surface huge theological and ethical problems arise from this encounter. Certainly God does appear to Job and for some commentators (e.g. Rowley, 1970) that is the key factor. But it is what he actually says – or rather does not say – that is the problem. As we will see below, Job is faced with a tirade of questions about his whereabouts at creation to which no human being would ever have any kind of answer. The issues that Job raised in the Dialogue about undeserved suffering are simply not addressed. There emerges a God in this situation who sets himself above the level of human beings, beyond any ethical responsibility towards them. The impression is of a God of power who can create great and wonderful things but who is not engaged with human dilemmas in the slightest way. The irony is that here he seems to be engaged more with non-humans, notably wild animals. Power seems to subsume any kind of justice. As Miles puts it, 'The Lord presents himself, with withering sarcasm and towering bravado, as an amoral, irresistible force. But Job has never called the Lord's power into question. It is his justice of which Job has demanded an accounting.' (1995: 315) Miles puts his finger on the key disjunction in the relationship here – Job demands justice whilst God simply stresses his power. Miles argues that God deliberately 'changes the subject' because 'he has no choice – he has subjected a just man to torture on a whim.' (Miles, 1995: 315) One could argue of course that it is Job's assumption that the world runs on justice that is his mistake and that to assume such is to limit God. This line is taken by Tsevat, who argues that God is saying to Job that retribution, as he has assumed it, is not what makes the created universe tick and that divine justice itself is a figment of the human imagination. God transcends justice – 'He Who speaks to man in the Book of Job is neither a just nor an unjust God but God.' (Tsevat, 1976: 105) One might argue that although the speeches of God do seem to stress power over justice, they are also about the sheer wonder, beauty and non-conformity of the created world. J.W. Whedbee calls it 'a playful festive note in the portrayal of creation' (Whedbee 1977: 24). Are we as human beings able to cope with the idea that God's world has dimensions that are beyond our experience or even our comprehension (e.g. 38.26)? The foundation of God's power is knowledge, understanding and ultimately wisdom itself, which is not neces-sarily identical to human wisdom. Indeed the wisdom enterprise is built on the foundation that God's ultimate wisdom is beyond human understand-ing and grasp (cf. chap. 28) and so there should be room in the human world-view for God's otherness and seeming lack of rule-keeping.

The relationship is two-way and Job's responses to God are the other side of the coin. Some scholars argue that Job gets the 'upper hand' over God at least in terms of morality. Miles writes, 'Ultimately Job wins: the Lord bows, in a way, to Job's characterization of God, abandons his wager with the devil and after a vain attempt to shout Job down, atones for his wrongdoing by doubling Job's initial fortune.' (Miles, 1995. 327) According to Miles, it is ironically God who learns more about the relationship with humans from this experience than Job learning more about God. However this is not the older scholarly opinion which generally saw the God speeches as some kind of corrective to Job from which he learns. Perhaps he was too self-concerned and self-centred (Peake, 1904) or perhaps he tried to intel-lectualize the situation too much (Kraeling, 1938). Nor is it the predomi-nant modern opinion that Job was right to protest against apparent injustice despite what God ultimately said, or didn't say. His actual responses indi-cate a humility before God – he first vows to be quiet (40.3-5) and then he acknowledges God's superior power and knowledge uttering his own confi-dence that he can challenge God and that experience of God is ultimately different to hearsay (see the key text in the next chapter). Maybe Job's only answer has been the experience of the divine and the fact that God did ultimately appear to him. Perhaps the experience is an emotional, intuitive religious one rather than an intellectually satisfying one. Is this the ultimate answer to the God/human relationship? If it does nothing else the book of Job certainly raises the 'big' questions of life!

4. Job: A Tragedy?

Of all the books in the bible, the book of Job comes closest to being a contender for classification as a tragedy. We are most of us aware of the great Greek tragedies, such as Aeschylus' *Prometheus Bound* (an interest-

ing parallel to Job, see J. J. Slotki, 1927-8 and K.J. Dell, 2007) and even
more so of the great Shakespearian tragedies of Hamlet, King Lear, Othello
and Macbeth. Job can be regarded as a tragic figure in that he has all the
makings of a tragic hero. He is a wealthy, respected, powerful man who is
inexplicably (for him) brought low so as to find himself sitting miserably on
a dung heap. He nobly rails against a seemingly hostile God and his only
so-called friends, who, after society and his wife have abandoned him, give
him more grief than succour. He develops an obsession with himself, with
his sickness and with the thought of death and ends up in despair, railing
against the universe. James Barr writes of the radical nature of Job, 'Though
he does not 'curse God' the preference for death is itself something verging
on the blasphemous.' (1971. 45) So far so good, and yet there are three fac-
tors in the book that spoil this picture – the first is God's appearance, the
second is Job's capitulation and the third is his ultimate restoration, as I will
discuss below. In a real tragedy the hero takes his own life and misses the
very restoration that is ordained for him. So does this mean the comparison
is void? As with most comparisons, the fit is not absolute, but the act of
making it reveals an aspect of the piece that had not come to light before.
It is my belief that making this comparison draws out some interesting
theological points. It also links up with my interest in genre as indicated in
chaps. 2 and 3 – here is a genre which may or may not have been known to
the author of Job (and the balance of probability is not in any formal literary
sense, or in relation to any particular historical connection – see discussion
in Dell, 2007) but which the book mirrors closely. Could we indeed see Job
as a forerunner of the development of 'the tragic figure'?

Some scholars are of the opinion that one cannot speak of tragedy and
religion in the same breath because of the God element. Belief in a just and
all-powerful God and in much suffering and evil being due to human freedom are inimical to the tragic worldview. Ultimate salvation, such as comes
to pass in the Job epilogue, is not a factor in tragedy. Indeed tragedy could
be seen as anti-religious in the way it exalts the tragic hero to a level more
sublime than the powers of fate or nature (which tend to replace belief in
any particular god) that he opposes. Indeed if the powers of fate are identified with God then humanity is seen to be overreaching itself and verging on
blasphemous behaviour. On the other hand if human beings decide to humble themselves in the face of God, as Job does in his final responses, that too
spoils the tragedy genre, where the dignity of the hero in the face of hostile
forces is a key ingredient. However, it is a fact that tragic heroes often face
the same kinds of problem that occur for religious people, notably for innocent sufferers such as Job – difficult moral dilemmas arise in both situations.
Issues about suffering and evil forces feature and questions about the nature
of some kind of power beyond human control are held in common.

If we turn to Job, looking at the book through the tragic lens, it is clear that were we to base our assessment on the Prologue and Epilogue alone – i.e. on the 'story' – there would be no tragedy. It is only the Job of the Dialogue who is a contender for tragedy, the more profound character who rails, protests and has moments of downright impiety when he accuses God of cruelty. And it is only the God of the God speeches who is a corresponding contender to represent the power of fate that is found in tragedy. A distant power that seems to be hostile, even playful, fits the bill of determining spiritual force outside human control. R.B. Sewall argues for a 'Hebraic tragic vision' which he finds primarily in Job. He argues that the author of Job saw the tragic possibilities of the story and opened it up so that the tragic element became clear – that there was no cause for his suffering and no satisfactory explanation. The only answer was a hostile God and a hostile universe, an answer in many ways affirmed in the God speeches where justice for humans appears to be of no concern to the deity. Have we uncovered here a dark side of God (see Barton, 2010), a God who is a dangerous mixture of power and capriciousness which tends to eclipse justice? Regarded in this light, the gap between tragedy and religion starts to close as God is seen to be as unpredictable as the dark forces of fate found in tragedy. And yet what ultimately spoils the tragedy is first God's appearance which suggests that the universe is not a hostile and empty place after all; second Job's humbling of himself even though his questions have not been answered (unless, of course, we see his 'repentance' as tongue-in-cheek) and third his vindication by God (42.7) which seems to contradict all that has gone before. Unless this is a parody of a tragedy, one that is deliberately undermined and spoiled, Job fails to pass this genre test. And yet, I would still hold that the comparison is instructive and illuminating.

Other suggestions have been made for Job – that it is a dark comedy (Whedbee, 1977); that it is instructively compared to 'horror' genres (Schlobin, 1992); that it is a work of deep irony (Good, 1965) and that its keynote is ultimately not tragedy but 'scepticism' (Dell, 1991). Perhaps at the end of the day what the author of Job is doing is raising questions for his audience to contemplate rather than attempting to provide definitive answers. In the manner of the Greek sceptics who themselves raised endless questions but found few, if any, answers, and indeed decided that truth was to be found in the questions and not the answers, the author of Job gives us different ways of looking at the world depending on how we read the book. If we read just the simple tale of the pious Job accepting what comes to him and finally being restored, we get a very different 'answer' to all the major theological themes – disinterested righteousness (certainly), retributive justice (yes, in the end) and the relationship between God and humanity (suffered a 'wobble' but all right at the last) to a reading that forefronts the

Job of the Dialogue and the God of the speeches, as we have seen. It is as if
the author is throwing up the questions, enjoying the disjunctions, delight-
ing in his parody and leaving his bewildered audience to take from it what
they will. In the next chapter I will turn to differing interpretations of Job
from very varied 'audiences' and perhaps, in true postmodern vein, that is
ultimately where Job's theological key lies – with the reader.

5. *The Yahweh Speeches and Job's Responses*

There are two Yahweh speeches – the first from 38.1-40.2 followed by Job's
first response and then the second from 40.6-41.34. Some scholars have
argued that the second Yahweh speech is a 'nagging extra' and that it has
a rather different character to the first and so must be a secondary addition. But that idea has largely fallen from favour today. The placing of the
speeches after the speeches of Elihu is perhaps curious in that one might
have expected them to follow immediately on from Job's reply. However,
wherever the speeches are placed, they do form the climax of the book.
Job's final plea had been for God to answer him and unexpectedly God does,
even if God does not appear directly to answer Job's concerns. The emphasis on God's creative acts is strong in these speeches and forms the focus of
the imagery contained within them.

Chapter 38 opens with God answering Job out of a whirlwind and posing
a series of rhetorical questions, i.e. questions to which he is not expecting
an answer. God too, interestingly, begins his speech talking about words –
this time Job is accused of speaking words without knowledge. This sounds
like a rebuke from God. God's opening question 'Where were you when I
laid the foundation of the earth?' (38.1) puts Job in his place. Of course
he was not there at the beginning of the creative act – Wisdom was there,
according to Proverbs 8.22-30. Perhaps there is the inference here that Job
does not have wisdom in its fullness in the way that he would like to think
he does. The series of questions continues – does he know the measurements of the earth and how it was put together? Did he control the waters
of chaos and prescribe bounds for the sea? Does he control the cycle of the
day and night? Even in this description of creation there is mention of the
wicked who are shaken out of the earth by God like one shakes a cloth. The
righteous/wicked nexus is part of the order of the earth and of society. The
earth itself changes at daybreak – its colours change in the way that a dye
changes a garment. But the wicked are happier in a realm of darkness, away
from the light. When they rise up they are quickly cut down.

The questions continue, and they serve as a vehicle for describing God's
acts in creation, the foundation of the earth and sea, God's control of the
cycles of light and dark, the ordering of righteous and wicked and God's

knowledge of the furthest recesses of the earth (cf. chap. 28). Has Job been to the place where the sea begins or to the depths of the sea? Has he been down to the very gates of the realm of the dead? Does he even realize the expanse of the earth? Of course the answer to all these questions is 'No' – God is using this technique to make Job realize that there is so much that he does not know. He has dared to challenge this great God who can do all things. Does Job know where light and darkness have their source? The inference is that Wisdom does know these things and so does God, but humans have their limitations. Human life is limited in both its knowledge and span – Job would have had to have lived a long time to have known all this. There is a heavy note of sarcasm in the accusation 'Surely you know, for you were born then'. One needs to remember that knowledge of the workings of the world was limited then – this poem reflects some of these limitations, although it is in fact a marvellous witness to all people had observed in those early times. The idea that the snow was kept in a storehouse ready for God's use, as also hailstones, is reflected in vv. 22-4. The idea of all the elements having a source somewhere in the physical realm is another primitive idea.

Rain and thunder are all in the realm of God's power – God is responsible for all fertility in the ground. The passage describes dew, ice and hoarfrost, also with their beginning in God. The stars are then described – does Job know their times and seasons? The greatness of God's works is stressed over and over again here – God's greatness rather than God's justice. The elements are under God's rule and command. God can send floods or lightning. Can Job do these things? From the external creation we move then to human beings – who has put wisdom inside a person? Of course the answer is still God, not Job. Only God knows how many clouds there are and how to make it rain. Again, a primitive belief in God tilting the clouds so that water spills out of them to make it rain is revealed. Rain then affects the earth and makes for the clods that hold the earth together – the description here is very observed and detailed. The knowledge of the created world that is coming across here is profound and strangely poetic and beautiful. At verse 39 of chap. 38 the interest turns from the earth and heavens to the animals that live on the earth and this is reflected throughout chap. 39. This chapter ends with a description of the lion and the raven. God provides for all the animals – these needs are not noticed by human beings but God sustains them in every detail.

In chap. 39, God is in charge of times and seasons. God knows when goats high up in the mountains give birth, and when timid deer produce their calves. God sees every detail of the process and the wonder of the birth and sustenance of these young animals is attributed to God's care. This description of wild animals that are largely outside human control and outside the human domain gets across the idea that God cares for creatures other than humans, and on God's own terms without humans needing to be there to control things. Job had wanted to control his understanding of the world too much – his mind was too limited. God's care for the world extends well beyond mortals to include wild asses and oxen. God provides for their wellbeing, God nurtures their instincts and delights in their differing natures. The wild ox is outside human taming – it is wild and unreliable, useless to humans and yet God delights in its creation. The ostrich behaves in a way unacceptable to human understanding in the way it lays eggs and then leaves them; maybe it shows a lack of wisdom, at least in human terms, but it is a proud member of God's creation, part of the otherness of his untamed creative world. In verse 19 we are on more familiar ground with the horse, whom humans can tame. However this description gets across the horse's pride and fearlessness in the face of battle. This description is an exaltation of the species, again perceived to be the way it is because God made it so. Job is asked too about the hawk – does it soar thanks to Job's wisdom? Of course not – this again is the realm of God. Great, strong birds too are at God's command and appear to behave at odds to human norms, and yet God has deliberately made these animals the way they are, different to humans. The world does not revolve either around humans generally or around Job in particular is the message here. The speech ends in 40.1 with a challenge from God to Job to respond.

It is at this point that Job reacts simply to assert his smallness in the face of God's might. For once he seems to be speechless. His act of laying his hand on his mouth suggests that he has nothing more to say beyond what he has already said and this is the gist of his words. Is this an ironic, tongue-in-cheek response at the blustering of the Deity? Some have read it this way. Others see it, at face value, as a genuine humbling in the light of God's power.

The second speech of God commences in 40.6. God begins his speech with the same words as in the first speech 9 (vv. 6-7) but then varies the accusation to Job, that he has tried to put God in the wrong and justify himself over God. This is along the same lines as Elihu's accusation of Job. Verse 9 reminds Job again of God's power. Isn't it clear that Job has nothing like the strength of God? The questions continue in the next verses – who is as majestic and glorious as God? Who has the same capacity for anger? Who can tread the wicked in the dust? The answer is implied – no human being, only God. All that Job can do is learn and submit to God.

This is where the long descriptions of primeval beasts comes in, beasts that have links to real creatures – the hippopotamus and crocodile respectively – but which also represent the primeval creatures of chaos that needed to be overcome by God. From 40.15 there is a long description of the Behemoth, which most closely resembles a hippopotamus and it is described in superlative terms, with a particular emphasis on its strength. It is also however described as 'the first of the great acts of God', like Wisdom, hinting at the primeval creation where God overcomes a monster representing chaos (which is still, according to this text, created by God). It is powerful and fearless and king of the beasts – only God can overcome it. The question in verse 24 suggests the answer 'no' – no one can catch it in a snare. In chap. 41 we turn to Leviathan, the crocodile, with the same thought – can anyone ensnare it? Can Job do these things? The description of Leviathan is almost humanized in vv. 3-4, but in fact it shows God in relationship with animals not just with human beings. It is not going to be Job's servant, only God's. There is no way that it can be caught and sold on to traders. Only God can control its mighty strength. The Leviathan has terrible teeth and skin like chain mail. The imagery is rich here and it gets across the frighteningly powerful nature of this beast. It sounds like a dragon with fire issuing from its mouth and nostrils. Although it is recognizable as a crocodile, the description goes beyond simply that, to describe the most frightening creature imaginable. Swords and other weapons simply bounce off its back. Here God's role in overcoming this creature is not stressed, although the divine ability to do so is understood. Rather, emphasis is on the power and terror it embodies – again, it is a creature beyond human understanding and represents the realm of God's activity.

This seems to be enough to humble Job in 42.1-6. He acknowledges God's power and the range of his activity. He knows that God is all-powerful. He cites God's words and says that he has 'uttered what I did not understand'. He has seen a glimpse of the heavenly realm. He still wishes to address God, though, and uses the opening remarks about hearing and speaking that we have by now become familiar with. His excuse here is that seeing God has made a difference to him – he had only previously heard about God second-hand. There is something in the appearance that satisfies him. Perhaps the appearance of God means more to him ultimately than what God actually said, which was hardly a direct response to his issues. However, Job does claim to have reached a deeper understanding, and that is presumably through what God has said to him. Job ends with a self-deprecating word about himself – he hates himself now for behaving as he did and abases himself in the dust and ashes with which he has become so familiar. Some scholars have suggested that this so-called repentance is rather 'tongue in cheek', that Job is simply cowering under God's powerful presence but realizing that he has in fact won the argument. This would be an interesting ironic twist, but may be reading too much into his words here. His experience is the key in my view – he had heard of God only what others told him, now he has experienced the divine for himself. He thought he had knowledge, but it was only partial.

Bibliography

Works Cited

Y. Hoffmann, 'The Relation between the Prologue and the Speech-Cycles in Job:
    A Reconsideration', *VT*, 31 (1981), pp. 160-170.

C. Jung, *Answer to Job*, 2nd edn (London: Routledge & Kegan Paul 1979).

R.N. Whybray, 'Shall Not the Judge of All the Earth Do What Is Just?' God's
    Oppression of the Innocent in the Old Testament' in *Shall Not the Judge of All
    the Earth Do What is Right? Studies on the Nature of God in Tribute to James L.
    Crenshaw* (ed. D. Penchansky and P. Redditt, Winona Lake, IN: Eisenbrauns,
    2000), pp. 1-19.

W. O. E. Oesterley and T H Robinson, *An Introduction to the Books of the Old
    Testament* (London: SPCK, 1934).

M. Weiss, *The Story of Job's Beginning* (Jerusalem Magnes, 1983).

M. Tsevat, 'The Meaning of the book of Job', *HUCA*, 37 (1966), pp. 73-106;
    reprinted in R.B. Zuck, *Sitting with Job* (Grand Rapids MI: Baker Book House,
    1992), pp. 189-229.

A. Lacoque, 'Job and religion at its best', *Biblical Interpretation* 4 (1996),
    pp. 131-153.

C.A. Newsom, *The Book of Job: A Contest of Moral Imaginations* (Oxford: Oxford
    University Press, 2003).

J.D. Pleins, 'Why do you hide your face? Divine silence and speech in the book of
    Job' *Int* 48.3 (1994), pp. 229-238.

H.H. Rowley, *The Book of Job*, NCB (London: Nelson, 1970).

J. Miles, *God: A Biography* (London Simon & Schuster 1995).

J.W. Whedbee, 'The Comedy of Job', *Semeia* 7 (*Studies in the Book of Job*, eds.
    R. Polzin and D. Robertson) 1977: 1-39.

A.S. Peake, *The Problem of Suffering in the Old Testament* (London: Robert Bryant,
    1904).

E.G. Kraeling, *The Book of the Ways of God* (London: SPCK, 1938).

J.J. Slotki, 'The Origin of the Book of Job', *EXPT*, 39 (1927-8), pp. 131-135.

K.J. Dell, 'Job: Sceptics, Philosophers and Tragedians', in *Das Buch Hiob und seine
    Interpretationen: Beiträge zum Hiob-Symposium auf dem Monte Verita vom 14-19
    August, 2005*, AThANT, 88 (Zurich: Theologischer Verlag, 2007), pp. 1-19.

J. Barr, 'The Book of Job and its Modern Interpreters', *BJRL*, 54 (1971-2),
    pp. 28-46.

R.B. Sewall, 'The Book of Job', *The Vision of Tragedy*, 1959, pp. 9-24.

J. Barton, 'The dark side of God in the Old Testament' in *Ethical and Unethical
    in the Old Testament: God and humans in Dialogue*, ed. Katharine J Dell,
    LHBOTS, 528 (London: T & T Clark International, 2010), pp. 122-134.

R.C. Schlobin, Prototypic Horror, the genre of the book of Job', *Semeia* 60 (1992),
    pp. 23-38.

E.M. Good, *Irony in the Old Testament* (London: SPCK, 1965).

K.J. Dell, *The Book of Job as Sceptical Literature*, BZAW, 197 (Berlin & New York: Walter de Gruyter, 1991).

Further Reading

1. The Problem of Suffering

B. Blake, *The Book of Job and the Problem of Suffering* (London & New York: Hodder and Stoughton, 1911).

H.S. Kushner, *When bad things happen to good people* (New York: Schocken Books, 1981).

O. Leaman, *Evil and Suffering in Jewish Philosophy*, Cambridge Studies in Religious Traditions 6 (Cambridge: Cambridge University Press, 1995).

F.C. Hyman, 'Job, or the Suffering God', *Judaism* 42 (1993), pp. 218-228.

K.J. Dell, *Shaking a Fist at God* (London: Harper Collins, 1995).

2. The Problem of God in Relationship with Humanity

D. Cox, *The Triumph of Impotence: Job and the Tradition of the Absurd*, Analecta Gregoriana, 212 (Rome: Universita Gregoriana, 1978).

J.L. Crenshaw, *Theodicy in the Old Testament* (Philadelphia: Fortress; London: SPCK, 1973).

J.L. Crenshaw, *Defending God: Biblical Responses to the Problem of Evil* (Oxford: Oxford University Press, 2005).

T.W. Tilley, 'God and the Silencing of Job', *Modern Theology* 5 (1989), pp. 257-270.

M.V. Fox, 'Job 38 and God's rhetoric', *Semeia* 19 (1981), pp. 53-61.

K.J. Dell, 'Does God behave ethically in the book of Job?', *Ethical and Unethical in the Old Testament: God and humans in Dialogue*, ed. K.J. Dell, LHBOTS, 528 (London: T & T Clark International, 2010), pp. 170-186.

3. Tragedy

C. Exum, *Tragedy and Biblical Narrative* (Cambridge: Cambridge University Press, 1992).

G. Steiner, 'Tragedy, Remorse and Justice', *The Listener* 102 (1979), pp. 508-511.

R. Gordis, 'The conflict of tradition and experience', *Great Moral Dilemmas in Literature*, ed. R. M. McIver (New York: Institute for Religious and Social Studies, 1956), pp. 155-178.

H. Kallen, *The Book of Job as a Greek Tragedy Restored* (New York: Hill and Wang, 1959).

W. Irwin, 'Job and Prometheus', *JR*, 30 (1950), pp. 90-108.

D.D. Raphael, 'Tragedy and Religion', *The Paradox of Tragedy* (London: Allen & Unwin, 1960).

4. *Other*

A.G. Hunter, 'Could not the Universe have come into existence 200 yards to the left? A thematic study of Job' in *Text as Pretext: Essays in Honour of Robert Davidson*, JSOTS, 138 (ed..R.P. Carroll) (Sheffield: JSOT, 1992), pp. 140-159.

J.T. Wilcox, *The Bitterness of Job: A Philosophical Reading* (Ann Arbor: The University of Michigan Press, 1989).

T.F. Dailey, *The Repentant Job: A Ricoeurian Icon for Biblical Theology* (Lanham Md.: University Press of America, 1994).

'Reading' Job in a Postmodern World

Interest has focused in Old Testament study in recent years on the 'reader' of texts. There is a burgeoning literature on readers of present and past and how texts can be legitimately approached with different agendas in mind. This in turn has led to many new insights into the texts themselves which indicates that reading texts is not simply a subjective matter. In this chapter I am going to treat four major areas of 'readers' who have come to prominence in the last few decades, ending with a new suggestion of a type of psychological reading of Job. There are many more readings that could be pursued – David Clines (1989) in his commentary on Job shows how an economic/materialist reading might work and even how one can do a vegetarian reading! The possibilities are endless and it leads to the issue of what is and what is not an 'authoritative reading'. Are all readings equally valid, or are readings backed by tradition or by church or synagogue more valid than others? The huge variety of interpretations from the past, as well as the present, show us that there is no such thing as a pure, unbiased reading. Everyone has some agenda or another, whether they are aware of it or not. Attempts to be totally objective are doomed to failure, and yet complete subjectivity is also a step too far. A useful model in the context of this discussion is the hermeneutic circle of Paul Ricoeur by which every text has a certain objectivity that affects readers in similar ways but which is read differently by every reader and so gains a subjectivity in that context that in turn feeds back into an objective assessment of the text. Here we come outside the realm of authorial intention to view the text as a finished product and its impact on the reader as the prime concern.

1. Feminist Appraisals of Job

Job is not the first text one would tend to turn to for a feminist appraisal, largely because the female characters in the book are few and play a minor role. However a feminist approach should not simply be confined in biblical studies to reappraisal of female characters, as A. Brenner points out, 'Feminism is a worldview, a political statement.' (1995: 19) Her volume *A Feminist Companion to Wisdom Literature* (1995) remains the most thorough treatment of Job from a feminist perspective, and whilst some of the articles focus on the female characters in Job, most creatively on Job's wife (E van Wolde, 1995), other articles indicate other feminine concerns that can be brought to such a text. The language of the womb for example is a feature of the Dialogue, as drawn out by L.R. Klein (1995), which I will consider below, and the possible vestiges of goddess imagery in the God speeches is of interest to L.M. Bechtel, although her argument for such is weak, in my view.

Clines in his commentary on Job (1989) perhaps sums up what for me is the key issue here when attempting a feminist reading when he writes 'The major feminist question, however, for the book is whether its principal concern is in any way a gender-determined one. If it is at all difficult to imagine an alternative version of the book in which all the protagonists were female and in which at the same time the principal issue arising from the loss of family, social standing and reputation was the doctrine of retribution and the justice of God, then to that extent the book, however sublime a literary work, may be defective, as yet another expression of an uncritical androcentricity.' (p l (i.e. 50 in roman numerals)).

My response to this point is that the book of Job is on the whole accessible to male and female at its fundamental theological levels. Job is representative of suffering humanity, struggling to understand the human/God relationship. Whilst an all-female cast in Job might have very different emphasis, it is not impossible to imagine. In fact, it is often pointed out that we have no direct reaction to the loss of her children from Job's wife and that she would have felt the loss just as deeply, if not more so, as childbearer, than her husband. Perhaps her response of 'Curse God and die' (2.9) is her indirect reaction and expresses her bitterness, but the terseness of this statement does not betray many clues. Clearly there are issues of social status here that would not apply to a female, in that the world represented is one in which males have a higher social standing than females and would hence feel the loss of that standing more keenly. However, for women, social standing would largely be achieved through their husbands and so any fall from grace affecting one would affect the other.

Clines suggests that the book feeds the male outlook of the time that 'weighty theological matters are the preserve of males, and that women have no place in such discussions' (1989: l). This may have been true in the culture of the time, although we have evidence that there were educated women around in biblical times, not least through the wisdom literature itself, in Proverbs with the mother's teaching role and the capable wife of chap. 31. However, as readers, we are aware that the book has been speaking to males and females over the centuries and so in this sense, as the female role has expanded and equalized with the male, the book has been able to speak on profound theological levels to both sexes alike. It is true, as Clines also asserts, that Job's wife does not have the most positive role in the book – she is often likened to Eve as the temptress who incites her husband to a course of action that will only lead to his death; her words about cursing God echo those of the Satan figure in the Prologue and she is not developed as a character and hence is more of a foil to others than a real person in her own right. It is possible though to look at the whole situation through her eyes – filling in the gaps in the narrative, as feminist approaches often try to do – and seeing her grief at the loss of her ten children, her social standing (because her husband has lost his) and her 'lot' at now having a very sick and complaining husband on her hands! Interestingly this kind of gap-filling had already taken place in the Job tradition when interpreters were concerned about the lack of detail about Job's wife (see Dell (1991) chapter 1).

It is not really clear what her 'Curse/bless (Heb: *barak*) really means'. Is she angry and bitter with Job, wondering why he still insists on his precious 'integrity' in the light of events which now suggest only one thing – that he has sinned and must be punished? Or is she on his side, showing her loyalty in believing his integrity to be intact? Is she to be aligned with the Satan (also citing his words, wittingly or not) or the friends in the unquestioning adherence to the doctrine of retribution? Or is her contribution more to be likened to echoing God's words (which she literally does repeat in the first half of verse 9 – itself an irony that she uses God's words of praise about Job to express her own impatience with him)? Perhaps she is expressing her ultimate support for her husband in the sentiment that death would be a release in the face of such suffering. Or maybe there is some self-interest shown here in that if Job died she would probably be able to return to the security of her parental home, whilst in the present situation her societal security is as low as Job's. Ellen van Wolde (1995) argues that the ambiguity in Job's wife's response in relation to the meaning of the word *barak* (bless/curse) provides a key to understanding Job's own character development in the book. According to van Wolde, Mrs Job (as she calls her) could be saying either – she is offering him a choice between cursing God with the effect that God leaves him and this results in his death, or blessing God and still die (possibly as a result of suicide), but with blessing on his lips. Job of course does not take up her suggestion and appears to reject her words as those of a foolish woman. Yet Van Wolde argues that Job's second response, after his wife's words, has led him to an uncertainty that makes him see the problem from a human angle rather than a divine one (as in 1.21-2). She writes, 'His wife introduces death and awakens doubt in him' (1995: 205). She attributes all the doubt shown by Job to this change in his perspective, awakened by his wife's words. Despite her seeming irrelevance at the start of the Prologue in that she is not even introduced in the first five verses, Job's wife arguably takes on a very important role in the balance of the whole book.

Brenner picks up the point that Job's retort to his wife is to call her a
'foolish woman' which then causes her to appear as 'a foolish and negative
foil to her husband' (1995b: 57). This is clearly, she argues, how Job sees her
and as he presents her. Who exactly these 'foolish women' are is another of
the text's conundrums – perhaps they are the opposite to wise women, as
known from Proverbs' polarities of categories. Whether however the reader
of the text accepts Job's judgement of his wife uncritically is another matter.
We have already been told that his piety was more than scrupulous, so perhaps his intense religiosity is already providing some tension for the reader,
who may see Job's wife's words as actually a rather pragmatic response to
an over-zealous God-fearer. Brenner also draws attention to the fact that in
Job's final plea in chap. 31 Job says that if he has committed adultery 'then
let my wife grind for another, and let other men kneel over her' (31.10).
The sexual overtones are clear, says Brenner. She indignantly sees Job as
using his wife as an object of 'verbal barter' here and comments in a foot-
note, 'Not surprisingly, Job barters his wife off rather than his own self as
punishment/expiation for his denied transgressions.' (1995b: 57) However,
another reading is that what in fact Job is saying is that he definitely is
innocent and his avowal is such that he would even hold up his closest
relationship – his wife – as surety. He then condemns adultery, suggesting
that the whole idea is abhorrent to him. So rather than bartering his wife
here, I prefer the idea that Job is mentioning her in the context of it being
an impossibility for him to even contemplate. There is never any doubt
from Job of his affection for and loyalty to his wife, despite his calling her
a 'foolish woman' in the context of her non-agreement with his particular
religious stance. We might compare 19.17 where Job's concern is that he is
repulsive to his wife because his breath is loathsome.

Job's wife is not mentioned in the Epilogue, something Brenner sees
as arguably 'justified in terms of her previous behaviour' (1995b: 58), and
appears to have been written out of the story, except that we may assume
that it is she who bears the second set of children. Her absence is not
explained or justified and the idea that the daughters are a foil to the wife
here (Brenner 1995b) is a possibility. Indeed, the only other female characters in the story are the daughters of Job. Early on we are introduced to
them, alongside their brothers, engaged in the act of eating and drinking
on feast days. It is somewhat surprising that they are mentioned separately
in this context and that they are clearly fully involved in such activity as
unmarried daughters. They don't appear to own houses as their brothers do,
suggesting their unmarried status, but rather attend parties at the brothers' houses in a fairly open way. Job sacrifices on behalf of all his children,
as part of his extra-scrupulous behaviour, not just on behalf of the males.
The new set of daughters is mentioned in the epilogue and here we have

the surprising details of their names and of their inheritance. Two of the three have names that indicate beauty products, which seems to me to be another ironic flourish on the part of the author. Having lost children in tragic circumstances, would one really name a second set 'eye liner' and 'horn of eye paint'?! The names may of course serve to point to the beauty of the daughters, which is also mentioned. The separate inheritance is more surprising in that the culture of the time would not normally have singled women out for special treatment in this kind of context (cf. a parallel in Numbers 27.1-11; 36.1-12 with regard to Zelophahad's daughters). Clines (1989) suggests that the two ideas of their beauty and their inheritance are linked, but I would like to think that it is as Job's offspring and the object of his special regard that such a concession is made.

Brenner suggests that the women in the story 'have no independent status; their function is to relate to Job as wife and daughters' (1995b: 56). Whilst it is true that Job is the main character and so other characters play roles that circulate around him, I am not sure that it is as a function of being female that this is the case. It is true that they are not given names in the story, but this may be by virtue of their minor role as characters rather than their gender. The friends are all named, even Elihu, but then they all say much more. Although women are often not named in the Old Testament more widely, and that may well be a feminist issue, perhaps the more surprising thing in Job is that the final set of daughters are named and we are given detail about them that we are never given about any of the sons who are also never named.

Klein's article offers particular insights in the section on womb imagery in the book of Job. She points out that women are regarded as the agent of life in giving birth. – 'the womb frequently becomes a synechdoche for woman' (1995: 197), e.g. Job says in 3.11, 'Why did I not die at birth, come forth from the womb and expire?' There are a number of references to the womb in Job in 3.10-11; 10.18-19; 24.20 and 31.15. Whilst the mother's womb is referred to in 1.21 and 31.18, 19.17 looks like a male adoption of the imagery in the phrase 'sons of my womb' which is Job's claim that his wife's womb belongs to him, and 38.28-9 refers to the 'cosmic womb' of the masculine God. Klein's conclusion is somewhat negative when she says 'Significantly, both life and death are identified with the woman's womb, decried by males but claimed by both earthly man and the male God.' (1995: 199). However there is a more positive way at looking at this imagery. Its use can be seen as an acknowledgement by Job of the role of his mother's womb in bringing him to birth and of his wife's in giving him that most precious gift of progeny. Admittedly he wishes in chap. 3 that he had not been born and in that context uses imagery of the womb, but this is not a criticism of the process itself, rather it is an acknowledgement of his dependence upon his

mother for his life and of woman's role in giving life. Job's use of the phrase
'sons of my womb' in 19.17 often rendered (as NRSV) 'my own family' is in
my view simply an acknowledgement that his offspring are his as well as his
wife's rather than a takeover of the role. As for the 'cosmic womb', 38.28
simply describes the creative act in language familiar from the process of
childbirth, with the breaking of the waters before the child comes forth.
The idea of the ice coming from a womb is also a figurative way of taking
about begetting – in my view, the sense is a question about where the ice
came from rather than literally attributing a womb to God. There is a question also whether God is male, as Klein seems to assume, or whether the
godhead is deliberately non-gendered. Bechtel sees the 'feminine' aspect of
the godhead as 'the creative interfacing of oppositional forces...unified in
one continuous process' (1995: 225). Whilst I question whether one can
really attribute one set of ideas to masculine and one to feminine, the idea
that both genders are subsumed in the godhead sounds a reasonable one.

This study of gendered imagery is an interesting way forward for feminist
study and there is scope for extending it in Job and elsewhere. Feminist
hermeneutics has to a large extent 'come of age' in recent years, with the
explicit attack on the 'maleness' of the texts and contexts being put to one
side in favour of a more positive appraisal such as I have offered in response
to the writers I have cited. Rather than become angry at the patriarchy,
modern feminist hermeneutics tries to work within that context to draw out
favourable aspects of the portrayal of women, to fill in the gaps in the text
and to reappraise gendered imagery.

2. *Liberation Theology Reading*

Perhaps the most famous liberationist reading of Job is that of Gustavo
Gutiérrez in his 1985 (original Spanish)/1988 (in English) book *On Job:
God-talk and the suffering of the innocent*. This reading is a contextual one
that begins with the question, 'what does this book have to say to my context?' – in this case to the suffering poor in South America. In doing such
a reading, fresh insights are gleaned from the text and new interpretations
brought so that it is a dynamic and fresh approach. It is essentially a theological reading and, in part, a spiritual one. Gutiérrez writes, 'How are
human beings to speak of God in the midst of poverty and suffering? This is
the question the Book of Job raises for us. An upright man living a prosperous, happy life is reduced to wretchedness and sickness. The key question is
therefore: How will Job speak of God in this situation?' (1988: 12) He sees
Job as representative of human beings generally so that the wider question
is 'How, then, is a human being to speak of God and to God in the situation that Job must endure?' (1988: 12) The Latin American experience

is seen to resonate with Job's situation of undeserved suffering. Gutiérrez writes, 'Nothing can justify a situation in which human beings lack the basic necessities for a life of dignity and in which their most elementary rights are not respected.' (1988: 12) For Gutiérrez the key question is 'Are suffering human beings able to enter into an authentic relationship with God and find a correct way of speaking about God?' (1988: 15) Gutiérrez sees Job's quest to understand as an unfolding path along which two major shifts of viewpoint take place. The speeches of the friends help to broaden Job's perspective so that he sees that the issue is not just his own suffering but that of all the poor. His task then, as a believer, is to lighten the burden of the poor by expressing solidarity with their plight. The second shift is occasioned by the God speeches: 'Job now understands that the world of justice must be located within the broad but demanding horizon of freedom that is formed by the gratuitousness of God's love.' (1988: 16) Gutiérrez characterizes these shifts as the language of prophecy and the language of contemplation respectively. He finds the ultimate key to the questions raised in Job in Job's second reply to God, which focuses on God rather than himself, and which enables us 'to see what the true relationship is between justice and gratuitousness; this, in my opinion, is the key to the interpretation of the Book of Job.' (1988: 82) This reply is based on an understanding of God's speeches that give him an answer – not the one he was expecting and yet an answer all the same. God's 'answer' according to Gutiérrez releases Job from the contradiction between his own experience and the doctrine of retribution because in facing up to it he gains release. Another aspect of Job that Gutiérrez brings out is Job's new preparedness to speak out and on behalf of an often unconfident poor that have not yet found their own voice. Gutiérrez stresses that the answer Job has found is one that is 'beyond justice' – 'The truth that he has grasped ... is that justice alone does not have the final say about how we are to speak of God. Only when we have come to realize that God's love is freely bestowed do we enter fully and definitively into the presence of the God of faith...God's love, like all true love, operates in a world not of cause and effect but of freedom and gratuitousness.' (1988: 87) In reference to the situation of the poor, Gutiérrez argues that God 'has a preferential love for the poor not because they are necessarily better than others, morally or religiously, but simply because they are poor and living in an inhuman situation that is contrary to God's will... The God of utter freedom and gratuitousness who has been revealed to Job can alone explain the privileged place of those whom the powerful and the self-righteous of society treat unjustly and make outcasts' (1988: 94) This is where the need to speak to the context of the poor of his society leads Gutiérrez to interpret Job more in that light and where, it could be argued, the reading strains the interpretation.

It is perhaps questionable whether Job in his arguments with the friends broadens out the situation to talk of the suffering poor in general and it is certainly questionable whether God has a special preference for the poor in quite the way that Gutiérrez describes here. To read the discourses with the friends in a 'prophetic' light is immediately reading those texts with the values of the prophetic literature, which do have a predilection for the poor in many places, at the forefront. If all readings are valid, then this one is particularly powerful for this situation. However, perhaps the greatest irony here is that Job is actually, to start with, a rich man who falls on hard times and his suffering is exacerbated by his loss of the status that he once enjoyed. He never knew what it was to be poor, and although he has lost everything and is arguably now one of the poor, he is in a rather different category from them in that he is a man brought low rather than one who never knew prosperity. Clines (1994) argues that the book of Job is a bad dream by a rich man about losing everything, and this gets across the point that I am making here. Job is not the first place that one might think to start for a liberationist reading – and Gutiérrez himself acknowledges that at the start of his book – and whilst it lends itself to profound insights for this kind of context, there is an element of distortion of its original intent and context that is perhaps inevitable and perhaps ultimately desirable if 'praxis' is one's key motivation in reading a text. That premise too, however, is questionable..

3. *Ecological Readings*

Ecological readings are another hermeneutical tool for unlocking aspects of biblical texts, but with a clear agenda that relates to the modern world. Again, the benefits are two-way in that new insights are brought to texts and illuminate them and yet the texts are used in the service of a voice that needs to be heard in the modern world. The Earth Bible project pioneered by Norman Habel has done a great deal to put the ecological agenda on the biblical studies map. His and Shirley Wurst's *The Earth Story in Wisdom Traditions* (2001) was the first clear attempt to deal with the book of Job within these terms of reference. The book is fertile ground for such an approach with its interest in creation and nature as particularly evidenced in the speeches of God in chaps. 38-40. However the agenda in this volume is specifically to look for the 'voice of earth', i.e. for Earth's own perspective (as personified by the capital 'E', rather than 'the earth') rather than human or divine evaluations of it, although the voice of Earth can speak through those of other characters. Habel himself argues that, in a reversal of traditional cosmology, Job depicts Earth as a place where suffering human beings are hounded by God – is he speaking for Earth in this sentiment too? Alice Sinnott's (2001) essay on Job 12 shows how the later part of the chapter (vv. 13-25) challenges God's governance of Earth and portrays God himself in less than positive terms. However in vv. 7-9 of the chapter the challenge is to ask the community of earth – notably the animals – to teach humankind, suggesting that Earth could itself become the teacher of humans. The God speeches are the subject of I. Spangenberg's article (1991) on Job 38-9 where God's concern for his whole creation is revealed, including his concern for wild animals. Spangenberg argues that there is a wisdom that God has implanted in wild animals that allows them to flourish far from human concern or intervention. As Dale Patrick (1981) argues, creation has worth apart from any human valuing of it, and that is an important message of the God speeches. Against Job's charges of God's tyranny in his governance of Earth, the God speeches defend the voice of Earth teaching the wisdom of the wild creatures and the role of God in his care for his creatures. Finally my own article on Job 28 shows how Wisdom becomes the intermediary between God, humans and Earth – is Wisdom's voice the same as Earth's here?

Another perspective is that which springs from the principles of Deep Ecology as I have argued elsewhere (K.J. Dell, 1994, 2010). These principles express the essential interrelatedness of God, humanity and the natural world. The first is concerned with nature's own complex processes and human interaction with those processes and with each other. Interaction with the divine is another key facet of this model, within the context of a theological worldview. The second concerns the well-being and flourishing of all human and non-human life in its richness and diversity. This includes ideas of the essential goodness of creation and awe at the sheer wonder of the created world. The third is that of the sustaining of life, the picture of God as creator in the Old Testament being essentially that of sustainer. One way in which the first principle is expressed in Job is in the delight that the wise had in likening unlike phenomena by joining them together in a proverb or question or observation. In Job such questions abound, e.g. 'Does the wild ass bray over its grass, or the ox low over its fodder?' (6.5) This suggests the answer 'no' since if these animals have their desire, which is food, there is no cause for complaint. Similes also feature in Job, as in this passage where Job's 'days' are personified, e.g. 'My days are swifter than a runner; they flee away, they see no good. They go by like skiffs of reed, like an eagle swooping on the prey.' (9.25-6) Metaphors are commonly found in Job, for example a ploughing metaphor used of the wicked: 'Those who plough iniquity and sow trouble reap the same' (4.8). Another technique is the use of personification of non-human elements to shed light on human life or experience. An example is the personification of day and night as witnesses to Job's conception and birth (3.1-10). Such examples show an

essential interaction between different facets of the world as experienced
and expressed by the wise.

A sense of awe at the created world – the second principle – is found in
Job 28, ostensibly a hymn to Wisdom, but arguably, rather, a hymn in praise
of the created world (see Dell, 2001). Precious metals are to be found in the
bowels of the earth and it is human ingenuity that finds them. The earth
readily provides 'bread' (v. 5) for human beings, but only its hidden depths
contains gold and fine sapphires (v. 6). By contrast to the earth, which
does ultimately reveal its treasures, Wisdom cannot be found at the highest
heights or deepest depths. There is a rich description here of the created
world, done with a sense of awe and wonder. Even great birds such as the
falcon and strong beasts such as the lion have not been able to find Wisdom.
Human beings probe all things yet no one knows the way to Wisdom. It is
not even in the 'land of the living' (v. 14) and the place of the dead has only
heard a 'rumour' of it (v. 22). It is not in the sea either, and it cannot be valued versus gold or glass. Its price is beyond coral, crystals or pearls, chryso-
lite or gold (vv. 16-19) all wonders of the earth in their own right. This list
of fine stones and metals is a description of the richness of the earth's gifts.
Although by comparison with all of these Wisdom is inaccessible, the point
of the description is to reveal these wonders and evoke awe. Human ingenuity is a part of this complex task to try to find Wisdom. Only God 'sees everything under the heavens' (v. 24) – God creates and sustains the wonders
of earth and heaven and so is the ultimate source of everything.

The third principle is the sustaining of life. This process is initiated by
God but continued by God's creatures who have a responsibility to the created world. God can choose to bring negative forces to bear as well as positive ones, and that needs to be remembered (e.g. 1.10) – this is echoed in
human maltreatment of the world. Job 38-39 describes wild animals created and sustained by God for no better purpose than personal delight. Not
everything is created for human benefit. Chapter 38 is structured as a series
of rhetorical questions to Job, designed to put him in his place. Was he
present at creation? The answer is, Of course not! God, by contrast, was and
what follows is a rich account of God's action in creation. Creation is both a
once-for-all act and a continuous process. The language of building is used
with terms such as foundation, measurements, stretching a line, sinking
bases and placing a cornerstone. God instills a sense of joy in the creation
(v. 7) as well as reining in chaotic elements to create order and harmony –
the sea needs to be shut in (v. 8) and bounded (v. 10). The day and night
have their own patterns and cycles. God's power is boundless (vv. 16-18,
19-21, and 22-24). God is also the provider of all sustenance – in vv. 25-27
and 28-30 of rain that waters the land and is the bringer of life to desolate
places far from human habitation. God controls stars, commands floods and

lightning and provides wisdom to humanity (vv. 34-38). Job 38.39 begins the long description of mainly wild animals created and sustained by God. Their habits are described, habits that are often inimical to human ideas of order (e.g. the ostrich's habit of leaving eggs unattended in 39.14-15). God has control of the cycles of their lives, those of lions, ravens, mountain goats, wild asses, wild oxen, the ostrich, the horse, hawk and eagle. These animals are untamed and free – like God. One gets a sense of the diversity and richness of non-human life from this description. All is dependent upon God – nature and God are in partnership in these chapters in a profound way, sometimes alienating the human perspective. This is a celebration of the wild and the untamed, of noble creatures nurtured by God but remaining wild. Job is not only overwhelmed with the wonders of creation, but he is urged to see other possibilities that lie outside a human-centred worldview and hence displace him from his usual 'world'. These speeches stress the beauty and non-conformity of the created world, they stress God's delight in his creation but also his power – as in the descriptions of Behemoth and Leviathan (40-41), great untamed creatures, set apart from human experience and control.

An ecological reading, then, takes our attention towards depictions of the created world and puts an emphasis on God as creator and humans as the recipients of all that the created world offers. The agenda of the reading is to emphasize those aspects that encourage a 'green' reading that enables human beings to nurture and understand and interact with the complex world around them. It is also to find the 'voice' of Earth and its creatures that may be lost on other readings.

4. A Psychological Reading

Thematic concerns have also been refreshed by an interest in Job from a psychological angle. Perhaps the most famous work on Job from a psychological angle was that of Carl Jung (1979) who deconstructed the figure of God in the book. For Jung, Job gets the better of God in that God reveals himself as a figure of power rather than one of justice. Jung writes, 'With the Job drama...Yahweh comes up against a man who stands firm, who clings to his rights until he is compelled to give way to brute force. He has seen God's face and the unconscious split in his nature. God was now known...' (Jung 1979: 54) Jung sees the real reason for God allowing Satan to inflict this suffering as a feeling of threat, a 'doubting thought'. He writes, 'It is amazing to see how easily Yahweh, quite without reason, had let himself be influenced by one of his sons, by a *doubting thought*, and made unsure of Job's faithfulness.' (Jung, 1979: 19-20) He goes on, 'This 'doubting thought' is Satan, who after completing his evil handiwork has returned to the paternal bosom in order to continue his subversive activity there.' (Jung, 1979: 26) By the time we get to the God speeches, Jung sees Job as seeing through the self-interest of God and realizing that there is no point in arguing with him. Jung writes, 'Job had noticed during this harangue [the God speeches] that everything else had been mentioned except his right. He has understood that it is at present impossible to argue the question of right, as it is only too obvious that Yahweh has no interest whatever in Job's cause but is far more preoccupied with his own affairs.' (Jung, 1979: 26).

Another possible reading is in the light of conflict theory and I will explore this here, building on insights of Leon Roper (2001) and others from my Job classes. P.D. Hanson regards the Bible as the 'source which has more to teach us about conflict and its resolution than any other.' (1985: 186-7) One thinks in particular of God's creative conflict with the dragon Leviathan, as also reflected in the ancient Near Eastern parallels. This 'reading' can be applied to the book of Job with some fruitful results.

There is a major conflict in the book between Job and God, and also between Job and the friends. In the prologue we come across an altercation between God and Satan on the topic of the motivation for Job's piety. Is it simply for reward, as Satan maintains, or is Job genuinely God-fearing? This is the opening conflict which is resolved by the test itself, but not until the conflict intensifies i.e. when Job passes part one of the test so that the Satan has to come back with part two – the infliction of the disease. It could be argued that Satan is the source of Job's conflict in the Dialogue as well as the Prologue, but since Job does not know that he blames God and so sets up the major conflict of the book between himself and God. Just before the end of the Prologue Job and his wife also disagree and so come into conflict – she tells him to 'Curse God and die' but he rebukes her as a foolish woman and will not accept her suggested response to God.

The Dialogue is full of examples of Job blaming God for his actions against him and he goes as far as to name God as his enemy (30.18-23). The previously reciprocal arrangement that led to Job's status, prosperity, friendships and family life has been replaced by a situation in which he has lost everything for no reason (since he is innocent) and hence lost his faith in the piety/prosperity nexus. At times he feels hunted and hedged in by God, at others he cannot find him – this reflects the fluctuating changes in the perception of the relationship with God that Job experiences in his stressed state. Job, in parodying fashion, accuses God not just of personal enmity, but of thwarting the very created order and corresponding social order that God set up in the first place. God is breaking the known rules of the wisdom world-view. Job is however powerless to control the situation – God has all the trump cards. His call in legal fashion for a response from God mounts as the Dialogue progresses and reaches its climax in chap. 31.

The conflict with the friends is borne out of Job's claim of innocence and his refusal to accept their evaluation of the act-consequence relationship. They urge repentance whilst he doesn't believe that he has anything to repent of. They urge submission which is the precise opposite of his intention. As the conflict increases so the barbed remarks and accusations mount between the two sides. Each is entrenched in their own position, the friends maintaining that Job's present circumstances are proof of his sin and Job claiming that this change in his fortunes is totally undeserved. Job finds the friends increasingly irritating and superfluous to his main argument (e.g. in 6.15-20 they are compared to a river that is treacherous in winter and disappears in summer, so useless to thirsty travellers), which is with God. The conflict between the two sides, like that with God, is both interpersonal in that there is intense rivalry between different characters and ideological in that they disagree fundamentally on a theological principle. Elihu too in his anger against Job shows his conflict with Job's rejection of traditional wisdom views. He is also critical of the friends for not having persuaded Job adequately, although he is essentially in agreement with them ideologically. A final conflict is found in the Epilogue when God sides with Job against the friends, although that is quickly resolved by Job's intercession on their behalf.

Having noted the conflicts in Job, it is at this point that ideas about conflict resolution as found in psychological theory might come into play as an interesting way of reading Job. Two attempts are made in the Dialogue to resolve the main conflict of the book, that between Job and God – one is by the friends and the other is by God. The friends suggest that the answer to resolving the conflict is for Job to acknowledge his guilt and repent. It is interesting that as Job gets increasingly annoyed with the friends, his conflict with God actually escalates rather than decreasing as they had hoped. The conflict is finally resolved by God – God appears and speaks and whether or not what God says satisfies him, Job replies in humble fashion. So God resolves a conflict that the friends have been unable to diffuse and this raises the question of the distinctiveness of God's approach versus that of the friends. The use of interactional theory (concerned with human family interactions) from psychology is of interest here. In such a family interactional context a therapist or mediator would be called upon to 'intervene', to help to resolve an interpersonal conflict (and it is interesting that Job in chap. 19 calls for just such a hypothetical mediator).

An important principle of psychotherapeutic intervention is support for the client (see M. Andolfi and C. Angelo, 1989). In order for change to occur, first there has to be a 'joining' attitude. The client needs to feel that their problem and its ramifications are fully understood and respected by the therapist. If an intervention is not supportive, then it becomes threatening to the client and may make the conflict worse rather than better. A first weakness of the friends' attempts to resolve the conflict is their essential lack of support for Job. Although in the Prologue they appear to sit in comforting and supporting silence during Job's grieving, by the start of the Dialogue, the criticisms of Job emerge. There is indeed a sense throughout the Dialogue that the friends are not really listening to Job but are repeating traditional positions. Their intention is help, not harm, but they prove less than helpful to Job by their attempts to convince him. They believe Job to be in the wrong and wish to persuade him so for his own good. However, they invalidate Job's own experience and his arguments springing from that experience, because of their fervour in putting forward their own position. It is no wonder that Job calls them 'worthless counsellors'! Job feels threatened by the fact that the friends are not listening to his point of view and he implores them to listen to him (e.g. 21.2). This frustration leads Job to turn his attention away from the friends towards God and his conflict with God, i.e. to the conflict that the friends' were trying (unsuccessfully) to resolve!

A second principle of psychotherapeutic intervention is that if two parties are caught up in circular arguments in a conflict, they need new information that will enable them to see the situation differently. D.S. and R.J. Becvar (1996) argue that in order to create alternative ways of looking at a situation, information that is new and meaningful, couched in a familiar language and world view, must be provided to both parties. The friends are guilty of being stuck in the rut of their own arguments, which, although differently nuanced, are essentially the same for the three of them. They are convinced that they are in the right and Job in the wrong, and their effect upon Job is to make him keep on reiterating his own points and insisting on his innocence. The positions become more hardened, as indicated by the increasingly frustrated tone of the Dialogue and by the insults that fly from one party to another. The friends try to change Job, but he just stays the same, and, if anything becomes more determined to vindicate himself. P. Watzlawick, J.H. Weakland and R. Fisch (1974: 22) call this process of a repeated pattern 'a game without end' and P. Watzlawick (1990) points out further that it is the 'attempted solution' that, ironically, maintains the conflict. In the book of Job, it is the 'attempted solution' offered by Job's friends that fails to resolve the issue as they go around in circles with their arguments. They cannot think outside the parameters of their own traditional wisdom position that the good are rewarded and the wicked punished.

A third principle of psychotherapeutic intervention is that those trying to intervene should avoid portraying themselves as experts. They should realize that we all have limitations on what we can know and that there are no certainties in life (the Becvars, 1996). The therapist should rather act as a 'perturber' and provider of new information. At the end of the day people decide to change themselves rather than being directly changed by others. It is clear that the friends think they are experts on retribution and hence that they know what is happening to Job – it is the result of his sin. The solution is to repent of sin and restore the relationship with God. This expert stance is frustrating to Job – he asks them to "keep silent" so that he focus on his argument with God (13.5) and he simply rejects their view. The problem here is the claim upon absolute truth that the friends put forward. They adhere to the belief that the doctrine of retribution is applicable universally and that there are no exceptions based on personal experience. Their duty then is to share this truth with Job in order to persuade him of his present misguidance. In fact Job himself believed in this very principle before his experience taught him otherwise and so he is not likely to go back to it!

Turning to God's intervention, which appears to change Job's attitude and can therefore be judged successful, three categories from psychoanalytical intervention theory can again be used. First is the fact that God's intervention is a second order intervention. Watzlawick, Weakland and Fisch (1974) make a distinction between first order change and second order change. First order change is when a logical solution is found within the rules of the relationship – this is the change attempted by the friends who try to use their logic to persuade Job. This may well be effective. Second order change however involves a change of the rules themselves and so in turn can change the relationship. On this model, the conflict is viewed differently and so new patterns of behaviour may emerge. The Becvars (1996), following others, compare second order change to a leap of imagination as experienced during moments of creativity. Watzlawick, Weakland and Fish argue that this kind of second order change is not always needed, but sometimes offers hope of a solution when change cannot be generated from within an existing relationship. God's intervention can be likened to this second-order change in that God behaves in a surprising way in that he sidesteps the retribution debate, focuses on the creation of the world, uses techniques of rhetorical questions and irony to address Job and takes him by surprise. Paul Dell (1980) writes, 'patterns can be changed by disrupting them' and this is what God does to Job. Just the fact that God actually does answer, contrary to expectation, and that answer is in dramatic fashion from a whirlwind throws Job into initial confusion. Then when God does not answer Job's questions directly, the sidestepping technique becomes clear. God's interests are different from those of Job and God's all-powerful nature is revealed. This is not a Dialogue between equals as before, this is a confrontation of unequals and Job in this new context drops his case, puts his hand over his mouth and submits to God.

A second principle from psychoanalytical theory, useful in this context, is that of provocation. A provocative intervention is one that, according to A. and N. Andolfi (1989), involves the therapist raising issues that are particularly meaningful within a relationship on an emotional level or airing views that have become entrenched on both sides. This would tend to bring emotional instabilities to the surface and often reveal the underlying cause of conflict. These issues are brought out in provocative fashion by the therapist by creating a crisis situation that attempts to generate an opening up of feelings and often a loss of control that disturbs the client's equilibrium. This provocative intervention then allows new forms of behaviour and encounter with others to be activated in the client. Thus change ultimately comes from within, on provocation, rather than being imposed from outside. In Job, the striking point about God's intervention is its lack throughout the Dialogue, which leads to the exacerbation of Job's pleas for God to respond to his case. God's lack of response also makes Job rethink the retribution principle and leads to his sense of having lost control of the order that characterized his previous life. Job's life now feels chaotic in the light of his lack of understanding of God's seemingly absent justice and a moment of crisis is on the cards. God's intervention in chaps. 38-41 arguably initiates this moment of crisis. There is from God no sympathetic agreement with Job or talking on his level, rather there is an increase of the tension in the avoidance of answering Job in the usual terms of the relationship. In the firing of unanswerable questions at Job, God succeeds in overwhelming Job and makes Job realize his smallness in the vast universe that God has created and is involved in sustaining. All he can do then is retract his words in 40.4 and 42.3.

A third principle harks back to the idea of support, but this time in the context of provocation. The Andolfis (1989) point out that no intervention can succeed without support. God certainly provokes Job but the question whether he provides support for Job at the same time is raised. A key point is that God does not blame Job for mounting his attack – indeed ultimately in the Epilogue at 42.7 he justifies Job over the friends. However, the nature of God's reply is to have accepted Job's challenge and to offer one in return that is somewhat off-centre. A second point is that God accentuates the power difference between the creator and Job, something of which Job has been acutely aware throughout the Dialogue (e.g. in 14: 18-20 Job accuses God of using his creative power destructively, thwarting human hope). For Job it made arguing with God seem almost pointless, but God, in meeting this point head-on, helps Job to come to terms with this difficulty. The Andolfis (1989) speak in terms of getting in touch with one's own suffering and feelings of inadequacy as being a way through a crisis. God's challenge to Job's fear of powerlessness shows a kind of empathy with where Job is at this point. The stress on God's power, often seen as bombastic, unnecessary behaviour, comes into focus on this theory as having an important role. A third point is that the stress on God's power in creation shows that God is in control and so restores Job's faith in an order that turns out to be different to what he thought, but at least is an order and provides security. The stress on God's creative role and sustaining of the universe demonstrates not only God's power but also God's unceasing concern for the created world. Andolfi and Angelo, (1983) make the point that clients appreciate the ability of the therapist to take control of the relationship and make them feel secure and supported.

Thus psychotherapeutic interactional theory can illuminate aspects of the book of Job that may have previously gone unnoticed by the scholarship. The language of intervention provides models for the responses of the friends and of God to Job and the theory highlights the differences between those responses that makes one end in failure and the other in success. The friends failed to adhere to significant principles of conflict resolution such as the provision of support to all parties, the avoidance of a circular dispute and suspicion of expert stances. God's intervention however fits into models of conflict resolution such as the taking on of a second-order or 'alternative' stance, and such as being provocative but also supportive. These kinds of models as applied to Job may enable the book to speak afresh to modern interpersonal conflicts of a similar kind and stimulate fresh readings of the book.

5. Job 42.7-17 The Epilogue

The final part of the book of Job is the Epilogue, usually treated as a pair with the Prologue, given that both are in prose and both have a folk-tale feel to them. After all the debate that has taken place over the doctrine of retribution, the placing of the Epilogue is somewhat ironic. As the friends had promised, Job is now restored. Perhaps his humble submission and acknowledgement of God's power and knowledge paved the way for this restoration, but somehow it has an unsatisfactory feel to it. The Epilogue opens with God rebuking the friends, addressing the first, Eliphaz, as representative of the three. Although it seems that the friends were right – that Job is now restored – they are told that they had not spoken right of God. This suggests that they had tried to limit God, to think that they had all the answers and to be fixed in their ways of understanding the situation. This is in many ways the key to the book, in that, had Job not been justified over the friends at this point, we would have thought that they were right and Job was wrong. Job being right suggests that to question God in the way that he did was better than to maintain traditional positions and that his protest – however radical – was worth making. Job is then instructed by God to perform a sacrifice on their behalf, with their bulls and rams. Job intercedes on the friends' behalf so that they are not punished. From verse 10 we have the restoration proper. Job is given twice as much in material goods. New characters – all his brothers and sisters – suddenly appear (interestingly his wife is not mentioned) and he is brought back into society. They give him gifts of money and gold jewellery. The numbers of animals are doubled, but the numbers of children are not. One might ask how satisfactory a replacement family would really be. Interestingly we are told the names of the daughters, their beauty is spelt out and the fact that they, unusually, are given an inheritance along with their brothers. Job is given long life and many offspring as the ultimate reward. No mention is made of the Satan figure at this point, which in some ways spoils the symmetry with the Prologue, nor is any mention made of the restoration of his health, although that is understood. So we have a happy ending after all – but in some ways this happy ending spoils the profundity of the book. However, we might ask how else the book could have ended – maybe this is the final flourish of the genius of this author.

Bibliography

D.J.A. Clines, *Job 1-20*, WBC (Dallas TX: Thomas Nelson, 1989)

A Brenner (ed.), *A Feminist Companion to Wisdom Literature* (Sheffield: Sheffield Academic Press, 1995).

A. Brenner, 'Figurations of Woman in Wisdom Literature' in *A Feminist Companion to Wisdom Literature* (ed. A. Brenner, Sheffield: Sheffield Academic Press, 1995), pp. 50-66.

E. van Wolde, 'The Development of Job: Mrs Job as Catalyst' in *A Feminist Companion to Wisdom Literature* (ed. A. Brenner, Sheffield: Sheffield Academic Press, 1995), pp. 201-221.

L.R. Klein, 'Job and the womb: Text about Men, Subtext about Women', in *A Feminist Companion to Wisdom Literature* (ed. A. Brenner, Sheffield: Sheffield Academic Press, 1995), pp. 186-200.

L.M. Bechtel, 'A Feminist Approach to the Book of Job' in *A Feminist Companion to Wisdom Literature* (ed. A. Brenner, Sheffield: Sheffield Academic Press, 1995), pp. 222-251.

K.J. Dell, *The Book of Job as Sceptical Literature*, BZAW, 197 (Berlin and New York: Walter de Gruyter, 1991).

G. Guttiérrez, *On Job: God-talk and the suffering of the innocent* (New York: Maryknoll, 1988).

D.J.A. Clines, 'Why is There a Book of Job and What Does It Do to You if You Read It?' in *The Book of Job*, Bibliotheca ephemeridum theologicarum lovaniensium 114 (ed. W.A.M. Beuken, Leuven: Louvain University Press, 1994).

N.C. Habel and S. Wurst (ed.), *The Earth Story in Wisdom Traditions* (Sheffield: Sheffield Academic Press, 2001).

A.M. Sinnott, 'Job 12: Cosmic Devastation and Social Turmoil' in *The Earth Story in Wisdom Traditions* (ed. N.C. Habel and S. Wurst Sheffield: Sheffield Academic Press, 2001), pp. 78-91.

I. Spangenberg, 'Who Cares? Reflections on the Story of the Ostrich (Job 39: 13-18)' in *The Earth Story in Wisdom Traditions* (ed. N.C. Habel and S. Wurst, Sheffield: Sheffield Academic Press, 2001), pp. 92-102.

D. Patrick, 'Divine Creative Power and the Decentering of Creation: The Subtext of the Lord's Addresses to Job', in *The Earth Story in Wisdom Traditions* (ed. N.C. Habel and S. Wurst, Sheffield: Sheffield Academic Press, 2001), pp. 103-115.

K.J. Dell, 'Plumbing the Depths of Earth: Job 28 and Deep Ecology', in *The Earth Story in Wisdom Traditions* (ed. N.C. Habel and S. Wurst, Sheffield: Sheffield Academic Press, 2001), pp. 116-125.

K.J. Dell, 'Green Ideas in the Wisdom Tradition', *SJT*, 47/4 (1994), pp. 423-451.

K.J. Dell, 'The Significance of the Wisdom Tradition in the Ecological Debate', *Ecological Hermeneutics: Biblical, Historical and Theological Perspectives* (eds. D.G. Horrell, C.Hunt, C.Southgate and F. Stavrakopoulou (London: T & T Clark International, 2010), pp. 56-69.

C. Jung, *Answer to Job*, 2nd edn. (London: Routledge & Kegan Paul, 1979).

L. A. Roper, *Conflict and Conflict Resolution in the Book of Job* (unpublished M. Phil thesis, University of Cambridge, 2001).

P.D. Hanson, 'Conflict in Ancient Israel and its resolution' in *Understanding the Word: Essays in honor of Bernard W. Anderson* (ed. J.T. Butler, E.W. Conrad and B.C. Ollenburger, Sheffield: JSOT, Press, 1985), pp. 185-205.

M. Andolfe and C. Angelo, *The myth of atlas: families and the therapeutic story* (New York: Brunner/Mazel, 1989).

D.S. Becvar and R.J. Becvar, *Family therapy: A systemic integration* (Boston: Allyn and Bacon, 1996).

P. Watzlawick, J. H. Weakland and R. Fisch, *Change: Principles of problem formation and problem resolution*, (New York: W.W. Norton, 1990).

P. Watzlawick, *Munchhausen's pigtail*, (New York: W.W. Norton, 1990).

P.F. Dell, 'Researching the family theories of schizophrenia: an experience in epistemological confusion', *Family Process* 19/4 (1980), pp. 321-335.

Further Reading

J. Chittester, *Job's Daughters: Women and Power* (New York: Paulist Press, 1990).

C.A. Newsom, 'Job' in The Women's Bible Commentary (ed. C.A. Newsom and S.H. Ringe, London: SPCK, 1992), pp. 130-136.

H. Cox, 'Complaining to God: Theodicy and the critique of modernity in the resurgence of traditional religion – Latin American Liberation Theology', *Archivio di Filosofia* 56 (1988), pp. 311-325.

Artists, novelists, playwrights and musicians have all been inspired by Job and here is a small selection of books/articles on the subject (for a much fuller bibliography, see D.J.A. Clines *Job* (WBC, Dallas TX: Thomas Nelson, 1989 and 2011).

S. Terrien, *The Iconography of Job through the centuries: Artists as Biblical Interpreters* (University Park, PN: The Pennsylvania State University Press, 1996).

N.A. Francisco, 'Job in World Literature', *Review and Expositor* 68 (1971), pp. 521-533.

M. Friedman, 'The Modern Job: On Melville, Dostoïevsky and Kafka', *Judaism* 12 (1963), pp. 436-455.

Muriel Spark, *The Only Problem* (London: The Bodley Head, 1984).

A. MacLeish, *J.B. A Play in Verse* (London: Secker & Warburg, 1959).

R. Vaughan Williams, *Job: A Masque for Dancing* (London, 1930 – musical score).

K.J. Dell, 'The book of Job in the English choral tradition' in *Leshon Limmudim: Festschrift for Andrew Macintosh*, eds. D. Baer and R.P. Gordon (forthcoming 2013).

K.J. Dell, 'The Book of Job in nineteenth century British oratorio' in *Festschrift for D.J.A. Clines on the occasion of his 75th birthday*, eds. J.K. Aitken and C. Maier (forthcoming 2013).

K.J. Dell, 'Twentieth century British and American Job oratorios' in *Festschrift for C.L. Seow*, eds. C. Yoder and S. Jones (forthcoming 2015).

C.L. Seow, 'Hope in two keys: musical impact and the poetics of Job 14' in *Congress Volume, Ljublijana 2007* (ed. A. Lemaire, VTS, 133, Leiden and Boston: Brill: 2010), pp. 495-510.

N.N. Glatzer, *The Dimensions of Job: A Study and Selected Readings* (New York: Schocken Books, 1969).

Index of Authors

Index of Subjects